The Concise Guide to Licensing

Ian Webster
TD MBA MRICS MIOL

The Concise Guide to Licensing

Matador
9 De Montfort Mews
Leicester LE1 7FW, UK
Tel: (+44) 116 255 9311 / 9312
Email: books@troubador.co.uk
Web: www.troubador.co.uk/matador

The publishers have made every effort to ensure the accuracy of
information presented in this publication. However, they can accept no
responsibility for any financial loss, or physical loss, injury or inconvenience
sustained by any reader as a result of information contained in this book.

ISBN 978-1906221-386

Cover design: Clare Daniels

Typeset in 10pt Plantin Light by Troubador Publishing Ltd, Leicester, UK
Printed by The Cromwell Press, Trowbridge, Wilts, UK

Matador is an imprint of Troubador Publishing Ltd

This book is dedicated to Mathew Pink, a former editor of Patterson's, colleague and true gentleman who passed away in 2006 following a life dedicated to the licensing profession.

Contents

Preface

This book is designed to provide a single concise guide for a range of licensing regimes. It is designed for those involved in licensing such as licensing officers, practitioners, police officers, fire officers, environmental health officers, surveyors, planners, councillors, applicants and licensees.

Each author has been involved with all chapters of the book however Ian Webster took the lead on chapters 1, 2, 3, 4 6, 8, 9 and 10, Jeffrey Leib on chapters 7 and 11 and James Button on chapter 5. Phil Easteal from Basildon DC Council (previously Thurrock) provided valuable expertise on the topic of animal licensing and Jim Hattersley on disabled access.

References

The book is designed as concise guide to the law. In writing it, we have drawn upon a number of other works, in particular, but not exclusively, three existing books which each provide a comprehensive and detailed reference work, namely:

- Taxis - Licensing Law and Practice, Button 2003 [ISBN 0406952825] (Button)
- Licensed Premises Law & Practice, Philip Kolvin et al 2004 [ISBN 1-84592-023-6] (Kolvin) and Supplement (Kolvin*)
- Alcohol & Entertainment Licensing Law, Manchester , Poppleston and Allen 2005 [ISBN 1-85941-672-1] (Manchester)

Licensing Practitioners

The book contains the syllabus for the National Certificate for Licensing Practitioners (NCLP) and candidates for this qualification should focus on chapters 2 (Policy) , 3 (Licensing Act), 8 (Hearings) and 11 (Enforcement).

Councillors

The book is also designed for the busy Councillor appointed to the Licensing Committee. Chapter 2 is designed to help with the development of policy and chapter 8 provides guidance on hearings.

Feedback

We would welcome feedback on this book to ensure future editions meet your needs. We would therefore be obliged if you could spend a few minutes completing the form page at www.LGS.uk.com

Foreword

The legislation currently in force in this England and Wales relating to licensing goes back over 150 years. Unfortunately there is no consistency in the Acts of Parliament. Each piece of legislation lays down different requirements for applications, various grounds for refusing an application or revoking a licence. This means anyone involved in licensing has to refer to a wide range of publications in an effort to find the answer to a query. There are many excellent books on licensing but they are usually specific to one area of licensing. Consequently a lot of time is spent researching in an effort to find the answer to a particular issue or locate sufficient information to point people in the right direction to find the answer. For a long time people involved in licensing have been asking for a concise, clear publication that will serve as a "one stop shop" to summarise legislation, give people an overview of the law and guide people in the right direction if they need more in depth information. In my opinion this excellent publication fills the gap.

The three authors have many years experience and knowledge of licensing and are well known and respected in licensing circles. They have provided a superb overview of licensing legislation and helped to explain the law and practice clearly and concisely. This book will help licensing officers, police officers, councillors, solicitors and anyone else involved in licensing with an excellent guide through the many varied corridors of licensing. I would recommend that this publication should become an essential part of the bookshelf of anyone involved in any part of the licensing process.

Roger Butterfield MIOL CSLP
Solicitor

1

History of Licensing

Throughout history the state has exercised control over certain activities and uses of buildings. This is particularly true for the sale of alcohol, gambling, public transport or any other activity which may endanger the public.

Such control is normally applied at the start of such operations through planning permission (development control) and in many cases continues with "ongoing" control through a licence or permit system. In covering the topic of licensing we will focus on the laws which provide ongoing control as distinct from development control and planning permission (although planning permission is briefly covered in Chapter 10).

The Oxford dictionary defines a licence as *"a permit from an authority to own or use something"* and a permit as *"an official document giving permission to do something"*. Such controls have existed in many societies for thousands of years. In 2300 BC, Hammurabi, King of Babylon introduced the first recorded laws which included controls on the sale of alcohol, an offence of allowing disorderly conduct in a tavern and the first building regulations. The offences were considered by independent hearings and the punishments rather harsh. Disorderly conduct in a tavern meant the taverner could be slain and the same fate awaited a builder if he built a house which collapsed killing the owner.

The state also has a history of getting involved in some of these controlled activities. Around 100BC the Hun Dynasty created a national lottery based on keno, a game of chance similar to bingo, to raise funds to pay for the construction of the Great Wall of China and the first lottery in England was introduced by Queen Elizabeth I in 16th century to raise funds to repair the Cinque Ports in Kent and East Sussex, which defended England.

Just prior to Queen Elizabeth's lottery Edward VI introduced the first regular licensing of the sale of alcohol (beer) in 1552 with the Alehouse Act. The purpose of the law was to help prevent disorder with the ongoing licensing of premises by the Justices. In the 17th century the state introduced the licensing of hackney carriages and sedan chairs with London issuing 300 licences in 1654. In 1847 the Government introduced the Town Police Clauses Act 1847 which is the current legislation controlling taxis outside Greater London.

When gin became the nation's favourite tipple, and drinking reached epidemic proportions, with crime and death rates rising, Parliament passed the Gin Act in 1729. The Act placed high duties on gin and resulted in large-scale illegal production and widespread protests. A new Gin Act in 1751 strengthened retail controls through a licensing system and drunkenness declined, with coffee and tea often taking the place of alcohol. At the same time licensed premises controls were introduced through the Disorderly Houses Act 1751 and in 1828 the licensing laws were consolidated into the Licensing Act 1828.

The United Kingdom introduced the first legislation for animal welfare in the world. In 1822 an Act was introduced to prevent the cruel and improper treatment of cattle. In 1951 The Pet Animals Act required the licensing of pet shops and during the 1960's kennels and riding establishments followed.

A major reform of liquor licensing occurred in 1869 and in 1914 further restriction was introduced to curtail drinking and enhance the war effort. The law restricted evening opening to 9.30pm and gave powers to military authorities to close pubs. In the north west of England authorities took control of four breweries in Carlisle as well as 235 pubs as there was concern over the effectiveness of the munitions workers due to drunkenness. Similar measures were introduced in parts of London and Scotland.

The alcohol licensing laws were further revised with the introduction of the Licensing Act in 1964 which continued with the concept of national restrictions on licensed premises exercised through the Courts. The same period saw the introduction of the Betting, Gaming and Lotteries Act 1963, the Gaming Act 1968 and the Lotteries and Amusements Act 1976, all recently superseded by the Gambling Act 2005 (GA05).

Within Greater London, the London Government Act 1963 (S52 and Schedule 12) gave the greater London Council (and from 1986, the London Boroughs) powers to licence public entertainments. Outside London, the largely similar provisions of the Local Government (Miscellaneous Provisions) Act 1982 (S1 and Schedule 1) placed the responsibility with District and Metropolitan Borough Councils (and from 1996, Unitary Authorities and Welsh County and County Borough Councils) to licence venues for public entertainment and the "primrose guide" laid down certain standards for existing buildings The latter Act also contained adoptive provisions to control some outdoor events.

Licensing of football stadia has also followed a clear path of tragedy, starting with the Ibrox stadium disasters of 1902 and 1971, Wembley in 1923 and Bolton in 1946, to the Bradford city football club fire of 1985 and the Hillsborough stadium tragedy in 1989. Consequently Parliament enacted the Safety of Sports Grounds Act 1975, amended by the Fire Safety and Safety at Places of Sports Act 1987.

As history shows, a key feature in virtually all licensing is the protection of the public and some licensing regimes have been introduced following a disaster. More recently the licensing of adventure activities was introduced in 1996, following the deaths of four school children in a canoeing accident in Lyme Bay and firearms licensing changed after the Dunblane massacre. The licensing of gangmasters was introduced after a group of more than 30 cocklers were caught in rising tides in Morecambe Bay with the loss of 19 lives in 2004. , leading to the establishment in 2005 of the national Gangmaster Licensing Authority (GLA). Pressure and concern over the conduct of largely unregulated nightclub doormen and a campaign by Dr Phyllis Starkey MP led to the Private Security Industry Act 2001 and the Security Industry Authority (SIA).

Applications under the Licensing Act 2003 (LA03) started on the 7th February 2005 and existing licence holders were given six months to apply to convert their existing licences into the new system. At the same licensees could also seek to change their existing hours or activities with a "simultaneous variation". The vast majority of applicants chose to take advantage of this option typically extending their licence by a couple of hours. Some sections of the press also embarked on a campaign against the new law. The Daily Mail ran a number of stories under the headline "say no to 24 hour pubs" and such negative campaigning did have an impact. Chris Webb the Licensing Manager at Medway Council thought that *those "applicants who submitted applications late in the transitional period tended to face more opposition from neighbours than those submitted in June"*. The minister responsible for licensing, James Purnell stated that only a handful of pubs (546) had applied for 24 hour opening *"That is about 0.5 per cent of the 200,000 premises"*. A report which followed added *"although 24 hour drinking has been hyped by the media, it is only really a sideshow to a more profound series of changes in licensing"*.

Legislation and technical standards need to move with the times and develop to keep pace with both technology and public opinion. In 1999 the Government set up an independent review of gambling law by Sir Alan Budd to consider the regulation of gambling. The Gambling Review Report "A Safe Bet" was completed in 2001 and it made 176 recommendations. This led to the Gambling Act 2005 which required existing operators to convert their existing licences during 2007.

During their period in power the Labour Government proved to be a radical reformer of some key licensing laws. The introduction of the Security Industry Authority (SIA) and associated licensing, the licensing of alcohol and entertainment with the Licensing Act and the comprehensive changes in the gambling laws, including internet gambling have all taken place. A feature of recent licensing is a shift in responsibility away from local Magistrates' Courts to Local Authorities.

2

Council Policy

Prior to 1834 collective "Local Government" did not exist with local services being provided by a range of controlling boards (Drainage Boards and Paving Commissioners etc). The Municipal Corporations Act 1835 introduced directly elected corporate boroughs with a range of duties.

Councils work within powers laid down under various Acts of Parliament. Some are mandatory, such as the licensing of premises for alcohol, entertainment and late night refreshment (Licensing Act 2003) and others are discretionary such as private hire vehicles, street trading and sex establishment licensing under the Local Government (Miscellaneous Provisions) Acts of 1976 and 1982.

Central government policy on alcohol, entertainment and gambling policy is predominately co-ordinated by the Department for Culture, Media and Sport (DCMS), with significant input from the Home Office, Department for Health, and the Department for Communities and Local Government. Central government policy on taxi and private hire vehicle licensing falls within the remit of the Department for Transport; other licensing policy areas fall to areas such as the Department for Trade and Industry.

In addition Councils do have a general power, under S2 Local Government Act 2000 to do anything which they consider is likely to improve:

- The economic well-being of their area.
- The social well-being of their area.
- The environmental well-being of their area.

Other than this general power under S2 Councils can only generally operate within the limits of any discretion granted to them by law, and they may be structured in one of four ways:

- An elected mayor with executive powers.
- A leader and cabinet with executive powers.
- An elected mayor with an appointed Council manager.
- A committee system with a requirement for overview and scrutiny (smaller authorities).

There are many Council functions which depend on local policies. The resolution (final agreement and introduction) of policy is normally by the Council as a whole, with implementation formally delegated to committees or officers.

Policy clearly forms part of the decision making process. However policies need not be drafted in robust legal terms. It is important that policies convey what it is that the Council is seeking to achieve.

Tensions often occur when balancing local discretion and autonomy against a desire for national consistency and proportionality. During the Gambling Act (GA05) consultation for the policy regulations the DCMS stated that regulations were necessary to *"provide transparency, and to some extent, consistency, for persons wishing to apply for a licence or permission under the Act, whilst minimising the imposition of unnecessary financial or administrative burdens on licensing authorities and the industry, and enabling local circumstances to be reflected in licensing policy statements".*

The law may also require that policies contain certain defined information. Under S5 of the Licensing Act 2003 (LA03), there is duty on Licensing Authorities to prepare a statement of licensing policy, but the Act is silent as to the nature of the policy. The Government has depended on statutory guidance, issued under S182 (chapter 3), including advice on principles, need, cumulative impact and opening hours.

Conversely, the Gambling Act 2005 (GA05) has taken a different approach. The GA05 (Licensing Authority Policy Statement) (England and Wales) Regulations 2006 require that a GA05 policy includes:

- Description or map of the area.

- List of consultees.
- The principles that the Licensing Authority will use to designate a body in writing to advise it on the protection of children from harm.
- The principles that the Council will use to decide who is an interested party entitled to make representations against licensing application.
- Exchange of information with the Gambling Commission and others listed in the GA05 Schedule 6.
- Inspection and enforcement.

The Local Authorities Co-Ordinators of Regulatory Services (LACORS), which assists local authorities in co-ordinating their regulatory work, suggest that policy has four purposes:

- To advise elected members.
- To inform applicants.
- To inform residents.
- To inform a Court at appeal.

Policy is also of little value if it does not achieve a desired outcome. Policy is therefore part of the implementation of a plan of action or a strategy. It has been suggested (Hogwood & Gunn, Models of Policy Making 1984) that there are ten elements to successful implementation:

- Circumstances beyond control do not impose crippling constraints (eg Government deadlines).
- There is adequate time and resources.
- The required combination of resources above are available.
- That the policy is based on a valid cause and effect.
- The relationship is direct.
- There is a minimum dependency on external agencies.
- There is agreement on the objectives.
- The tasks fully specified in correct sequence (project plan).
- There is good communication and coordination.
- There is top level support, this would include Members.

Although policy is a critical part of the decision process a House of Lords decision (British Oxygen v Board of Trade 1971, AC 610) established that every application must be considered on its own merits. It is not generally possible for an application to be determined on the basis of policy alone. Lord Reid said *"The general rule is that anyone who has to exercise a statutory discretion must not shut his ears to an application"*. Under no circumstances must a local authority fetter its discretion when deciding something, and must consider every matter (in relation to licensing) on its own particular merits, but in the light of the policy. In other words, the policy is the starting point for consideration of a matter, and not the conclusion.

The development of new policy or the amendment of existing policy relating to licensing should include the following stages:

- Identify local issues and any existing policies i.e. planning.
- Identify local stakeholders.
- Clarify issues and preferred options.
- Formal discussion report to Licensing committee.
- Consultation.
- Feedback on consultation to Licensing committee.
- Develop final policy.
- Resolution by Council (or whoever has the policy making power within the Council).
- Evaluate and review.

Having identified the relevant "stakeholders" it is almost inevitable that there will be varying views. Each party will want the problem defined according to their assumptions, values and goals. This may lead to conflict.

The options offered in the consultation process must include discussion and comparison of all reasonable options. Where there is an explicit or an implied requirement to consult before a policy is adopted, the decision-making policy must conduct the consultation whilst the proposals are at the formulative stage: see R (on the application of Sardar and others) v Watford Borough Council QBD 2006. The Courts have established that Councils cannot discount realistic options prior to consultation R (on application of Montpeliers etc) v City of Westminster EWHC 2005 (Kolvin★ p31).

The LA03 S182 Guidance states that "appropriate weight" should be given to the statutory consultees although the guidance does not define how this is achieved. The Gambling Commission guidance also advises Councils, for their statement of principles under GA05, that they must give appropriate weight to the views of those consulted. In determining what weight to give particular representations in relation to any consultation, the factors to be taken into account include:

- Who is making the representations (what is their expertise or interest).
- What their motivation may be for their views.
- How many other people have expressed the same or similar views.
- How far the representations relate to matters that the Licensing Authority should be including in the particular policy being consulted upon.

In June 2005 Mr Justice Richards sitting in the Administrative Court considered an application brought by the British Beer and Pub Association (BBPA), the Association of Licensed Multiple Retailers (ALMR) and the British Institute of Innkeeping (BII). R (BBPA and Others) v Canterbury City Council has established that LA03 policy should be presented as relevant to the three specific stages of making a licence application i.e. in relation to Canterbury City Council's statement of licensing policy.

- Completing the application (Stage 1).
- Processing of application (Stage 2).
- Committee determination (Stage 3).

Whilst it is acceptable to state expectations in a policy the Judge was critical of the wording as it may mislead an applicant. When referring to the operating schedule he stated *"the Licensing Authority has no power at all to lay down the contents of an application and has no power to assess an application unless there are relevant representations"*. The Council added a section at the start of the policy which the Judge described as a substantial improvement. However he was still concerned saying *"There is a risk that applicants will focus on particular parts of the policy without taking the time to read the document as a whole"* he described the policy as *"over-prescriptive in a number of places"*. The Judge did not quash the policy as it would have meant an administrative nightmare for the Council.

There are well established legal principles on consultation. They require Councils to ensure that they identify all appropriate consultees and make sure that:

- They are provided with or have access to the draft policy.
- They are given time for consideration of the policy.
- They are given the opportunity to make representations.
- Councils give serious consideration to any such representations.

The Cabinet Office has introduced a Code of Practice for Government departments carrying out consultation (refer to www.cabinetoffice.gov.uk). Whilst this code is not a mandatory requirement for Councils it does promote good practice.

- Consult widely throughout the process, allowing a minimum of 12 weeks for written consultation at least once during the development of the policy.
- Be clear about what your proposals are, who may be affected, what questions are being asked and the timescale for responses.
- Ensure that your consultation is clear, concise and widely accessible.
- Give feedback regarding the responses received and how the consultation process influenced the policy.
- Monitor your department's effectiveness at consultation, including through the use of a designated consultation coordinator.
- Ensure your consultation follows better regulation best practice, including carrying out a Regulatory Impact Assessment if appropriate.

Recent legislation has prescribed the consultees, but other legislation does not do this. In situations where there are no statutory consultees, it is necessary for the Local Authority to identify potential consultees, but also to advertise the consultation exercise widely to ensure that no relevant person or body misses the opportunity to comment. The LA03 requires that before determining its policy Councils must consult the persons listed in S5. These are:

- The chief officer of police for the area.

- The fire authority.
- Local holders of premises licences.
- Local holders of club premises certificates.
- Local holders of personal licences.
- Businesses and residents.

The GA05, S349 lists the following statutory consultees:

- Police.
- Persons representing gambling businesses in the district.
- Persons likely to be affected.

If legislation defines the consultees these are the minimum persons who should be consulted. There is nothing to prevent a Council consulting additional bodies however the costs of this consultation will not be included in any Government cost recovery calculations. Councils will therefore have to fund the additional consultation themselves.

All policy must be subject to review to ensure that it is relevant, delivering desired outcomes and up to date. Both the LA03 and GA05 stipulate a review of policy after three years; in areas where there is no such stipulation, a policy of re-examining policies after two to three years is a very sensible approach.

For LA03 policies there are a number of legal cases which help to define the content and role of policy. Westminster City Council introduced the first policy on what they termed "stress areas". The Council considered that certain parts of their borough had reached full capacity for licensed premises. The Council sought to restrict any further licences by including a "presumption against granting" in their policy. The matter was considered by judicial review and Mr Justice Scott Baker considered the presumption was acceptable. Kolvin sums up the position following this case, as follows (Kolvin p121):

- Policy may state that it is to be overridden only in exceptional circumstances.
- Rational for policy may be stated in policy – where it is, exceptions must be directed to the rational.
- Policy may exclude particular exceptional circumstances.

- Appeal Courts are to apply policy as if they are the Licensing Authority, that is, they 'stand in the shoes' of the Licensing Authority when considering the appeal.
- Policy may not be challenged in the Court hearing the appeal. The correct way is by judicial review in the High Court, which must be commenced within three months of the date of the action being complained about.

The Courts have since considered the issue of "cumulative impact" in Wetherspoons v Guildford Borough Council EWHC 815 2006. Wetherspoons applied for a conversion and variation to extend hours to 02.00hrs at their Lloyd's No 1 outlet in Bridge Street, Guildford. Guildford Borough Council had adopted a special policy for this part of the City and following a representation from the Police and a hearing they rejected the later opening. Wetherspoons argued that the Council could only apply the policy to new applications and not to applications for an extension of hours. The Council argued that the policy was valid and relevant to the application.

The Court (Mr Justice Beaston) commented that *"Any tension between the policy elements favouring the lengthening of licensing hours and recognising the needs of an area in which there is a particular concentration of premises is not resolved by the [statutory] guidance. This together with the fact that there are other policy elements in the guidance suggests that the guidance does not preclude the application of a cumulative impact policy to an application to extend hours"*. He found that Guildford had properly adopted a cumulative impact policy and that the Licensing committee had been prepared to consider any exceptions to its policy and dismissed the appeal.

This case demonstrates the real tensions which exist with any licensing policy. The S182 Guidance alludes to a concept that if adopting a pragmatic approach based on evidence then there will be little scope for political variation. The management writer Mary Parker Follet would have described this as "the law of the situation" (Creative Thinking 1924) i.e. given all the facts everyone will arrive at the same decision. Whilst in today's political environment there is less of a clear distinction between "left" and "right" any development of policy by Members will inevitably include choices based on values and judgements.

Following the resolution of policy or the adoption of discretionary controls the law will occasionally require public notification, such as:

- Gambling Act policy: Local newspaper and web site two weeks before publication (one month before taking effect).
- Sex establishment licensing adoption: Local newspaper for two consecutive weeks 28 days before implementation.
- Licensing Act policy: No prescribed requirement.
- Street trading adoption: in a local newspaper at least 28 days before the proposal is due to take effect, and for two consecutive weeks once the decision has been made.

3

Licensing Act 2003

The Licensing Act 2003 (LA03) introduced the first comprehensive review of alcohol licensing in 40 years and consolidated a range of licences into one regime. The statutory guidance made under S182 of the LA03 states that in addition to the licensing objectives the key aims are:

- Better regulation to give business greater freedom to meet customer needs.
- Greater choice for customers.
- More family friendly premises.
- More live music, dancing and theatre.
- Regeneration of areas by a thriving night-time economy.
- The protection of local residents.

In describing the change Manchester et al say *"it represents a completely fresh start, takes an innovative approach to licensing control and prescribes a new legislative framework"* (Manchester p19).

Licensing Authorities

The LA03 provides a single integrated system for licensing premises which sell alcohol, provide entertainment or late night refreshment, through licences issued by Licensing Authorities. These authorities are the District/Metropolitan/Unitary Council for the area and they are defined in S3 as:

- District Council in England.
- County Council in England where no District Council.

- County or County Borough Council in Wales.
- London Borough.
- Common Council of the City of London.
- Council of the Isles of Scilly.

As a Licensing Authority the Council has a duty under S4 to carry out the functions of the LA03 with a view to promoting the licensing objectives, namely:

- Prevention of crime and disorder.
- Public safety.
- Prevention of public nuisance.
- Protection of children from harm.

Each objective does warrant some description. The prevention of crime and disorder includes any criminal offence or disorder. Manchester et al describes disorder as *"conduct that seriously offends against values generally recognised by society as being of a character likely to cause annoyance"* (Manchester p109). The Guidance makes it clear that the public safety objective relates to the *"physical safety of persons using the premises and not with public health"* (para 7.32) and that the public nuisance objective retains a broad common law meaning and could include low level nuisance affecting a few people as well as major disturbance affecting the whole community (para 7.40). Whilst debating this objective the Lords had requested an amendment to *"the prevention of unreasonable diminution of the living and working amenity and environment of interested parties in the vicinity of the premises balancing those matters against the benefits to be derived from the leisure amenity of such premises"*. The Government did not accept this amendment, retaining the original objective. The final objective, protection of children from harm, includes the protection from *"moral, psychological and physical harm"* (S182 Guidance para 7.48).

S4 states that when undertaking this duty the Licensing Authority "must have regard" to:

- Its own licensing policy.
- S182 Guidance.

Licensing policy was covered in Chapter 2. The S182 Guidance, produced by the

DCMS, seeks to provide an interpretation of the law and in the foreword the SoS states that *"This Guidance is intended to aid licensing authorities in carrying out their functions under the 2003 Act and to ensure the spread of best practice and greater consistency of approach"*. The Guidance was considered by Parliament and must be kept under review. The term "must have regard to", both the guidance and policy, means that they must be followed unless there is good reason not too. The Oxford English dictionary definition of "regard" is to give heed, pay attention, take into account, consider. The Guidance states (para 2.3) that Licensing Authorities may depart from the Guidance if it has been *"properly and carefully understood and considered"*. Similarly for policy para 2.4 adds that it is important to give full reasons if departing from policy. The Court of Appeal (R v Brent LBC 2002) considered the role of guidance issued by the Secretary of State for Education and concluded *"Any appeal panel which, albeit on legal advice, treats the Secretary of State's guidance as something to be strictly adhered to or simply follows it because it is there will be breaking its statutory remit in at least three ways: it will be failing to exercise its own independent judgment; it will be treating guidance as if it were rules; and it will, in lawyers' terms, be fettering its own discretion. Equally, however, it will be breaking its remit if it neglects the guidance. The task is not an easy one"*.

The first review of the S182 Guidance was carried out within one year of the start date of LA03 and another is imminent as this book went to press. On the 22 June 2006 the DCMS revised the Guidance to clarify a number of points, including:

- Personal Licence (PersL) applications must include a criminal record certificate.
- Designated Premises Supervisor (DPS) may supervise more than one premises.
- A reinforcement of the position that planning and licensing are separate regimes.

Delegations

Each Licensing Authority must also set out how the function will be delegated to either committees or officers, although S10 does not allow delegation to officers if relevant representations are received. The majority of Licensing Authorities have adopted the suggested delegations in the S182 Guidance below (para 3.63). S6 places a duty on the Council to establish a Licensing committee of between 10 and 15 Councillors and unlike most Council committees there is no requirement for political balance of this committee. S9 allows the Licensing committee to also establish sub committees of three members to determine individual applications.

Matter to be dealt with	Sub Committee	Officers
PersL	If police objection	If no objection
PersL with unspent convictions	All cases	
PL/CPC	If representation	If no representation
Provisional statement	If representation	If no representation
Vary PL/CPC	If representation	If no representation
Vary DPS	If a police objection	All other cases
Request to be removed as DPS		All cases
Transfer of PL	If a police objection	All other cases
Interim authorities	If a police objection	All other cases
Review PL/CPC	All cases	
Complaint irrelevant, frivolous or vexatious		All cases
Object for premises outside its area	All cases	
Police objection to a TEN	All cases	

Licences and Licensable Activities

The LA03 licensing regime is based on:

- Personal Licences (PersL), issued for ten years following criminal record check and relevant qualification.
- Premises Licences (PL), incorporating an operating schedule (OS).
- Club Premises Certificates (CPC), incorporating a Club Operating Schedule (COS).
- Temporary Event Notices (TEN), to allow small scale licensable events.

Licences are required for what S1 describes as licensable activities, namely:

- Retail sale of alcohol.
- Supply of alcohol by a club.
- Provision of regulated entertainment.
- Late night refreshment.

The first licensable activity is the retail sale of alcohol and S191 defines alcohol as any spirit, wine, beer or cider with a strength of more than 0.5%. The LA03 specifically excludes the following products from this definition:

- Perfumes.
- Flavouring and aromatic essences, such as Angostura bitters.
- Medicinal, denatured, methyl alcohol or naphtha.
- Liqueur confectionary.

The Act also allows alcohol to be provided as a lottery prize, provided it is in a sealed container (S175).

The retail sale of alcohol does not include trade sales (including sales to PersL holders or those holding a TEN) or sales to a club which holds a CPC. For registered clubs the subsequent "purchase" by a club member is also not technically a retail sale as the member already owns the assets of the club, including the alcohol. In these circumstances the drink is "supplied" however this supply is also defined within the second licensable activity.

For other descriptions of alcoholic drinks, below a strength of 0.05% they may be classed as "alcohol free" and below 1.2% they may be described as "low alcohol".

The LA03 prohibits the sale of alcohol from the following:

- Moving vehicles (S156).
- Trains, on the order of Magistrates (S157).
- Motorway services (S176).
- Garages (S176).

The third licensable activity is specified as "regulated entertainment" which the

LA03 (Schedule 1) defines as:

- Plays. Any dramatic or theatrical performance.
- Films. Any display of moving pictures, other than a simultaneous TV broadcast.
- Indoor sport. Any game or activity for competition or display in a roofed structure, including a tent (but not a structure with a roof that can be opened or closed).
- Boxing or wrestling (indoors or outdoors). Any contest or exhibition.
- Live or recorded music. Amplified or un-amplified, other than incidental or spontaneous events.
- Dancing other than Morris dancing (or dancing of a similar nature).
- Anything similar to any performance or playing of live or recorded music, or dancing.

To qualify as licensable this entertainment must be provided (with or without charge) for:

- The public or a section of the public or
- Club members or their guests.

Private entertainment events are not licensable unless the organiser is planning to make a profit from the event. Schedule 1 excludes performers only from the definition of organisers and whether actual profit is made is not a factor only the original intention. For instance a person could invite ten friends to a private event with a live band, which cost £100, charging each of his friends £10 to cover the cost of the band and no licence would be required. If under the same circumstances he charged £11 each or invited eleven friends then this would constitute licensable activity.

There is some debate over whether money raised for charity would fall within the definition of profit. Manchester et al conclude that *"with a view to profit should be interpreted so as to exclude money raised for charity through private provision of entertainment"* (Manchester p152). It is important to note that this relates to private events only.

Venues which hire out facilities for dancing or making music are in themselves licensable. The Guidance states that this would include, for instance, the provision of a karaoke machine in a public house (para 5.11).

The LA03 includes a number of exemptions to regulated entertainment namely, incidental music, spontaneous events, video advertising, church services, garden fetes and moving vehicles. There is also some discussion on the provision of pub games and when they fall within the definition of indoor sport. The S182 Guidance clearly states that *"normally (pub games) would not be played for the entertainment of spectators but for the private enjoyment of the participants. As such, they would not normally constitute the provision of regulated entertainment"* (para 5.15).

The final licensable activity is late night refreshment, which is the serving of hot food or hot drinks, to the public, for consumption on or off the premises, between 23.00hrs and 05.00hrs. The following operations fall outside of this definition:

- Hotels for residents and guests.
- Recognised clubs.
- Staff canteens.
- Charity provision, such as a "soup kitchen".
- Drinks from vending machines.

Premises Licence (PL) and Club Premises Certificate (CPC)

A PL or CPC is issued by the Licensing Authority and authorises one or more of the licensable activities. S193 defines premises as any place including open air venues, vessels, stationary vehicles or moveable structures, other than:

- An aircraft, hovercraft or train on a journey.
- A vessel on an international journey.
- A designated port.
- Royal Palaces and military establishments (including premises of national security).

It is for the applicant to define the premises to be used for licensable activities, and they can include single rooms in buildings, particular levels of buildings, parts of fields or recreation grounds, etc.

For internet, telephone or mail order sales of alcohol the premises are defined as the place where the alcohol is dispatched and not the call centre taking the order or payment.

Unlike the previous law, which required a named person, S16 states that in addition to a person (minimum age 18) business, clubs or charities may apply for a PL. The application is submitted to the Licensing Authority on a prescribed form with the following supporting information:

- Fee.
- Operating schedule (OS).
- Plan.
- DPS consent, if including sale of alcohol.

Clubs, which meet the criteria of "Qualifying Clubs" under Part 4 of the LA03, may apply for a CPC. The qualifying requirements are:

- A minimum of two days between nomination/application and membership (S62).
- The Club is established and conducted in good faith (S63).
- The Club has a minimum of 25 members (S62).
- Alcohol is supplied to members and guests only (S62).
- Purchase and supply of alcohol managed by elected committee (S64).
- No arrangements for anyone to receive payment/benefit based on sales or supply of alcohol (S64).

Clubs operating with a CPC are not authorised to provide licensable activities to the public or to let their facilities to the public however there are some benefits, namely:

- No need for a PersL holder to authorise sales of alcohol.
- No need for a DPS.
- Limited rights of entry for police and enforcement officers.
- Not subject to Magistrates closures under S160.
- Not subject to police powers under S161 for instant closure.

The LA03 (Premises Licences and Club Premises Certificates) Regulations 2005 (referred to from now as the Premises Regulations) provide the detail of the application process including forms and notices.

Operating Schedule

Kolvin et al. describe the operating schedule as *"a key plank of the reforms…it forms a vitally important part of the completed application form for a premises licence since it serves to indicate the basis upon which it is proposed that the premises will be operated"* (Kolvin p173). The OS provides a general description of the style/character of the business and details how the premises will operate. The OS must also include the following:

- Name and address of the premises.
- State the licensable activities and times those activities take place.
- Opening times for non licensable activity.
- If the licence is for a limited period, details of that period.
- Where sale of alcohol, nominate the DPS and whether sales are for consumption on or off the premises.
- Following a risk assessment the steps necessary to promote the four licensing objectives.

The OS is produced by the applicant, to provide information to those assessing the application, on the basis of the four licensing objectives. When granting a licence the Licensing Authority may attach conditions which are consistent with the information contained in the OS. The S182 Guidance states *"any individual preparing an operating schedule is at liberty to volunteer any measure …as a step he or she intends to take to promote the licensing objectives. When incorporated into the licence or certificate as a condition, they become enforceable under the law and a breach of such a condition could give rise to prosecution"* (Annex D).

The Premises Regulations prescribe the layout of an OS with the timings boxes allowing for non-standard or seasonal variation opening times. This may include opening linked to local or regional events or international sporting fixtures.

For premises selling alcohol then the OS must include the name of the person nominated as the DPS. The Guidance states that this person is normally the person with day to day responsibility for the premises and there can be only one such nomination on the licence (Guidance para 4.18). However, the Act does not specify any particular responsibilities for the DPS, and although they can commit certain offences, in each case the DPS must have "knowledge" of the situation. Any person specified as a DPS needs to be a PersL holder and due to the importance of this role and the responsibility that rests with them the Premises Regulations (R24) require that the DPS signs a declaration that they are willing to accept this legal position.

Plans

The Premises Regulations (R23) requires that the plan submitted with the application should be drawn to a scale of 1:100 and show:

- The boundary of the building, including walls and the perimeter of the premises.
- Entry and exit points and escape routes.
- If the premises are used for more than one licensable activity, the area for each activity.
- Fixed structures (including furniture) which may impact on escape.
- Any stage (including height) and any steps, stairs, elevators or lifts.
- WC's and kitchens.
- Fire safety equipment.

The plan may include a legend to cover the matters above by the use of symbols etc. and the Licensing Authority can agree in advance of the application to accept plans drawn to other scales.

Consultation

Copies of the application must also be served, on the same day (R27), to the following "responsible authorities", defined in S13:

- Police.
- Fire officer.

- Health & safety.
- Planning.
- Environmental health.
- Nominated body for protection of children
- Weights and measures (added by the Premises Regulations, R7).
- If the premises straddles the Council boundary, the other Licensing Authorities.
- For vessels the navigation authority.

The Premises Regulations (R25) require that the application is advertised as follows:

- Prominently displaying an A4, pale blue notice which can be conveniently read from the exterior of the premises for a period of no less than 28 days from the day after the day of the application, and
- By publishing a notice in a local newspaper within ten working days from the day after the day of the application.

For large sites or premises the pale blue notices must be displayed every 50m, along the boundary with a highway, although most Licensing Authorities adopt a pragmatic approach to this requirement for very large sites.

The Premises Regulations (R26) go on to say that in the case of an application for a PL etc the notices referred to in regulation 25 shall state the licensable activities (or relevant qualifying club activities) and include:

- The name of the applicant (or club).
- The address of the premises.
- The address (including the worldwide web address) of the Licensing Authority.
- The date by which an interested party or responsible authority may make representations.
- That representations shall be made in writing and
- That it is an offence knowingly or recklessly to make a false statement in connection with an application and the maximum fine for which a person is liable on summary conviction for the offence.

The purpose of these notices is to bring the application to the attention of "interested parties" who are defined in S13 as:

- A person, or body representing a person, who lives in the vicinity.
- A business, or body representing a business, in the vicinity.

Any person may then inspect the detail of the application, but only interested parties may lodge a representation. The decision as to whether a person is an "interested party" lies with the Licensing Authority concerned.

Determination

Applications must be determined in accordance with S18, which contains a "must grant" provision. The Licensing Authority has no alternative but to grant an application unless a responsible authority or interested party has made a relevant representation, in which case they must hold a hearing (refer to Chapter 8). Conditions can only be imposed on a licence if they are consistent with the OS or they are considered necessary following a hearing. There are three exceptions to this rule and Licensing Authorities must impose the following conditions if the OS includes selling alcohol (S19), showing films (S20/74) or employing door supervisors (S21). S22/S76 prohibits the Licensing Authority from attaching a condition to a PL/CPC to specify the type or content of a theatrical performance and S75 prohibits any condition restricting associate members of a club.

S19 (Mandatory Conditions). No supply of alcohol made be made under the PL:

- At a time when there is no DPS in respect of the PL, or
- At a time when the DPS does not hold a PersL or his PersL is suspended.

Every supply of alcohol under the PL must be made or authorised by a person who holds a PersL. This means that the PersL does not have to undertake every sale of alcohol, and indeed need not be present on the premises at all times that alcohol is being sold, but he remains responsible for such sales (Guidance para 7.67). Although not required by the Act, it is considered good practice that any such authorisation by a PersL holder should be in writing.

S20/S76 (Mandatory Condition). Where children are admitted to the exhibition of films, their admission must be restricted in accordance with the recommenda-tions of the Licensing Authority or a film classification body specified on the licence (usually the British Board of Film Classification).

S21 (Mandatory Condition). Where the PL contains a condition requiring the presence of persons carrying out a security function (Door Supervisors) such individuals must be licensed by the Security Industry Authority (SIA).

The PL or CPC layout is prescribed in the Premises Regulations, which stipulates that the Licensing Authority should issue of a full licence and a summary. The content of these documents is prescribed in Schedule 12 for a PL and Schedule 13 for a CPC and the main licence includes:

- Licence number.
- Premises details.
- Licence holder.
- Mandatory conditions.
- OS conditions.
- Hearing conditions.
- Plans.

Following the grant or refusal of a PL S23 requires the Licensing Authority to notify the following:

- The applicant.
- Any person who made relevant representations.
- The police.

Once issued the licence lasts until such time as:

- It is revoked (S52).
- The death, incapacity or insolvency of the holder (S27).
- The holder surrenders (S28).

Variations, Transfers and Interim Arrangements

Applicants may apply to vary the PL or CPC under S34/S84 or transfer a PL under S42.

Variation applications are processed and determined in a similar manner to a new application however they can not be used to "substantially" alter the building. Manchester et al conclude that for building alterations *"substantial variations require a new premises licence, middle range variations require a variation application and minor variations might be dealt with informally"* (Manchester p248).

A separate procedure exists to change the DPS nominated on a PL using S37. The Premises Regulations (R13) prescribes the content of the application which must be copied to the Police and the existing DPS. As with a new application the proposed DPS must submit a signed declaration of his acceptance to this position.

An existing DPS may also serve notice to be removed from the licence using S41. The notice is prescribed in the Premises Regulations and must be served to the Licensing Authority and copied to the licence holder, who must within 14 days return the original licence to the Licensing Authority. The premises will not be authorised to serve alcohol until the licence holder nominates a new DPS using S37 and S38 allows the change to have immediate effect.

A PL will lapse on the death, incapacity or insolvency of the holder or by its surrender. In such circumstances a person dealing with the estate may submit an interim authority notice under S47 or apply to reinstate the licence under S50. An interim authority notice must be served within seven days and is valid for up to two months, allowing the premises to trade until the formal transfer takes place. The licence may also be reinstated under S50 if the new holder is known at the time of the lapse. A S50 notice should also be served within seven days and copied to the police.

Applications under S37 (change of DPS), S42 (transfer), S47 (interim) or S50 (reinstate) do not need to be advertised or served on the responsible authorities other than the police.

Provisional Statements

Anyone proposing to build or substantially alter (including the change of use of a premises) may gain an assurance that the proposals are acceptable under the LA03 prior to development. An application may be made for a provisional statement under S29, and Schedule 3 of the Premises Regulations prescribes the content of the application which must include:

- Application form.
- Plans.
- Schedule of works.
- Fee.

The process is the same as a new application with the notice being served on responsible authorities together with site notices and public notices. The Licensing Authority must issue the statement unless relevant representations are received when a hearing must be held. A Provisional statement is effectively a statement of principle. Once the premises are ready to commence operation, an application for a PL must be made in the usual way. At this stage, S32 prohibits further representations on matters that could have been considered at the time of the provisional statement.

Opening Times

The concept of permitted terminal hour no longer exists. If representations are received it is for each Licensing Authority to determine the opening times for each premises based on the merits of the application.

The LA03 seeks to promote flexibility in opening hours, with a range of opening and closing times to suit customer demand. When considering hours of operation Licensing Authorities should not employ "zoning" (impose closing times in certain areas) or seek to engineer "staggered closing". For shops selling "off sales" the Guidance states (para 3.31) that the hours permitted on the licence will normally be granted to match the shops opening hours. This removes the need to stop selling alcohol whilst the shop is open on a Sunday morning, and can allow 24 hour off-sales from supermarkets.

Kolvin et al. conclude that *"on the basis of the current available evidence it is not possible to draw firm conclusions as to whether or not allowing later terminal hours will lead to a general reduction in levels of public disorder"* (Kolvin p665). However, at the time of writing, there have been no indications that the changes brought about by the LA03 have increased crime or disorder.

Small Venues

S177 of the LA03 takes the prize for gobbledegook and has obviously been drafted to achieve some compromise during the implementation of the law. In essence the section applies to "small venues" which are described as having a "certified" occupancy limit of 200. The section is designed in some way to replace what was known under the previous law as the "two in the bar rule" which automatically allowed holders of a liquor licence up to two live performers in their premises without the need for a Public Entertainment Licence. However, it fails to achieve this, as to take advantage of the S177 exemption, the premises must hold a PL allowing not only the supply of alcohol for consumption on the premises, but also musical entertainment.

Under S177, for small premises authorised for live music and dancing, any conditions attached by the Licensing Authority relating to public nuisance or protection of children are not active and if the live music finishes before midnight and is unamplified no imposed conditions apply to the licence.

Following a review hearing the Licensing Authority can "disapply" any rights under S177.

Personal Licence

A PersL authorises the holder to supply alcohol or authorise the supply of alcohol in accordance with a PL (S111). The licence is issued by the local Licensing Authority where the applicant lives (S117) and lasts for ten years (S115). To gain a licence the applicant must (S120):

- Be 18 or over.
- Possess a nominated qualification, as listed below.
- Must not have any "unspent" convictions for a "relevant offence" defined in Schedule 4 (as amended).
- Not forfeited a licence within five years.

The detailed procedures are prescribed in the LA03 (Personal Licences) Regulations 2005 (referred to from now as the PersL Regulations). Unless the police object the Licensing Authority must grant the application if it meets the criteria stated in S120. If the police object the Licensing Authority must hold a hearing, and the Guidance states that it will be normal for the Licensing Authority to refuse, unless there are *"exceptional and compelling circumstances"* (para 4.8).

The Government has accredited the following PersL qualifications under the LA03:

- BIIAB Level 2 National Certificate for PersL Holders (NCPLH).
- GOAL Level 2 Certificate for PersL Holders.
- GQAL Level 2 National Certificate for PersL Holders.

The content for the PersL qualification includes the following topics. The BIIAB state that the NCPLH *"is both QCA (Qualifications and Curriculum Authority) accredited and Government approved, and has been specifically designed to meet the statutory requirements of the Licensing Act 2003"*.

- Licensing authorities.
- PersLs.
- Alcohol.
- Unauthorised licensable activities.
- Police powers.
- Duties of the PersL holder.
- Premises licences.
- Operating schedules.
- Permitted temporary activities.
- Disorderly conduct on licensed premises.
- Protection of children.
- Rights of entry.

The PersL Regulations (R6/R7) prescribe the content of the application which includes:

- An application form.
- Criminal record certificate (maximum one month old).
- Declaration relating to relevant offences (PersL Regulations Sch 3).

- Two passport style photographs (one endorsed as a true likeness).
- Fee.

The relevant offences are listed in Schedule 4 (as amended by Licensing Act 2003 (Personal Licence: Relevant Offences) (Amendment) Order 2005) of the LA03 and they include:

- Licensing or PEL etc.
- Theft.
- Supply of drugs.
- Gaming.
- Customs and excise offences.
- Breach of copyright etc.
- Drink driving.
- Food safety.
- Sexual or violence offences.

A PersL holder has a legal duty to:

- Notify any Court they are a PersL holder (S128).
- Notify the Licensing Authority of any relevant convictions (S132).
- Notify the Licensing Authority of a change of address etc. (S127).
- Produce the licence (S135).

The PersL Regulations (R5) prescribe that the licence must include the issuing Licensing Authority, a photograph, ID number and be in a "durable" form no larger than 100mm x 70mm. Renewal applications must be made to the Licensing Authority which issued the original licence.

Children

The new system is keen to promote family friendly venues and clarifies the position relating to children on licensed premises. It is an offence to:

- Allow an unaccompanied child (under 16) on premises with a primary use of the supply of alcohol (S145).
- Allow an unaccompanied child (under 16) on licensed premises after midnight and before 05.00hrs (S145).
- Sell alcohol to children (under 18) (S146).
- Allow sale of alcohol to children (under 18) (S147).
- Sell liqueur confectionary to a child (under 16) (S148).
- Purchase alcohol by or on behalf of children (under 18) (S149).
- Consumption of alcohol by children (under 18)★ (S150).
- Delivering alcohol to children (under 18) (S151).
- Sending children to obtain alcohol (under 18) (S152).
- Unsupervised sales of alcohol by children (under 18) (S153).

The Guidance does offer advice on the issue of alcohol being a primary use *"The expression should be given its ordinary and natural meaning in the context of the particular circumstances. It will normally be quite clear that the business being operated at the premises is predominantly the sale and consumption of alcohol"* (para 3.34).

The Guidance (para 3.37) encourages Licensing Authority policy to highlight areas that will give rise to particular concern if children are to be permitted into a venue, namely:

- Entertainment of an adult or sexual nature.
- Where there have been convictions for serving alcohol to minors.
- Where drug taking or dealing is suspected.
- Where there is a strong element of gambling.
- Where the supply of alcohol for consumption on the premises is the exclusive or primary purpose.

Freeholder Interests

Any person with a freehold interest in a property with a PL may serve notice under S178 (Rights of Freeholders). This notice should be served on the

★ Although it is an offence for children to consume alcohol S150 does allow a 16 or 17 to consume beer, wine or cider with a table meal, if accompanied by an adult.

Licensing Authority and ensures that the freeholder is advised directly if the Licensing Authority are considering any action, such as closure of the premises. The notice should be served every year and a prescribed fee is payable.

Special Occasions

The LA03 (S172) allows the Secretary of State to declare special occasions when all premises will receive authority to open over a "celebration period" following a "Licensing Hours Order" which could extend opening for a period of up to four days.

Temporary Events

To replace "occasional licences" the LA03 (S100) introduces the concept of a "permitted temporary event" which the Guidance describes as "an exceptionally light touch bureaucracy" (para 8.2). Any event which will last less than four days (96hrs), with less that 500 people may use this process to authorise licensable activities by the serving of a Temporary Event Notice (TEN). The details of the notice are prescribed in the LA03 (Permitted Temporary Activities) (Notices) Regulations 2005 (Referred to from now as the TEN Regulations).

In addition to the limits on the duration and size of the event the LA03 imposes the following restrictions:

- Maximum 12 TEN or 15 days within a year for any premises (S107).
- Minimum of 24 hours between events (S101).
- PersL holders may issue a maximum 50 within a year (S107).
- Non licence holders may issue a maximum five within a year (S107).
- Applicant a minimum 18 years old (S100).

The content of the notice is prescribed in Schedule 1 of the TEN Regulations and the notice must be served on the Licensing Authority (two copies) and police, a minimum of ten working days before the event, excluding the day of the event. The Licensing Authority must acknowledge receipt of the notice under S102 within one working day.

As long as the overall limits detailed above are not exceeded, only the police can seek to stop a temporary event and then solely on the basis of crime prevention. If they consider the event would undermine the crime prevention objective they must serve a counter notice under S104 within 48 hours of receipt of the TEN to the:

- Licensing Authority.
- Applicant.

If the limits are exceeded, the Licensing Authority must issue a counter notice (S107).

Unless agreement can be reached between the applicant and the police the Licensing Authority must hold a hearing which must be completed 24 hours before the scheduled event. The Guidance states that at such a hearing the Licensing Authority *"is confined to the crime prevention objective. It may not, for example, uphold a police objection notice on the grounds of public nuisance"* (para 8.16). If Members conclude that the event would undermine crime prevention then the Licensing Authority must serve an objection notice under S104.

The premises user has a duty to display either a copy of the TEN at the premises, or a notice stating that the TEN is kept securely on the premises, and by whom (S109).

Licensing Register

Every Licensing Authority must maintain a public register, the contents of which are defined in S8 and Schedule 3 of the LA03 and the LA03 (Licensing Authority's Register) (Other Information) Regulations 2005. The register should include the following:

- Premises applications (S17), including OS and plans.
- Provisional statements (S29), including any schedule of works and plans.
- Variation of PL (S34).
- Change of DPS (S37).

- Transfers (S42) and interim authority (S47).
- CPC application (S71), including OS and plans.
- Variation of CPC (S84).
- Premises review (S51)/(S167) or CPC (S87), including grounds for review.
- PersL application (S117) or change of name/address (127).
- TEN counter notice (S105) or modified TEN (S106).
- Closure orders (S165).

Fees

The fees and charges are prescribed in the LA03 (Fees) Regulations 2005 (referred to from now as the Fees Regulations). For most types of new applications they are based on the Non Domestic Rateable Value (NDRV) of the premises, placing them into one of the following five categories, A to E (Schedules 1 and 2). Premises under construction fall in band C and premises without a rateable value pay the fee in band A.

Band	NDRV (£K)	Apply (£)	Annual (£)
A	<4.3	100	70
B	4.3 to 33	190	180
C	33 to 87	315	295
D	87 to 125	450	320
E	>125	635	350

Larger venues and events with a capacity of 5,000 or more are subject to additional charges. The Fees Regulations state that premises in bands D and E, where *"the premises is used exclusively or primarily for the carrying on on the premises of the supply of alcohol for consumption on the premises, the amount of the fee shall be"*:

- Band D, two times (applies to application and annual charge).
- Band E, three times (applies to application and annual charge).

Events over 5,000 also attract an additional fee, set out in Schedule 3, and annual charges are payable, which are set out in Schedule 5 of the Fees Regulations.

The Fees Regulations also exempt the need to pay fees for:

- Schools for regulated entertainment for school activity.
- Village halls for regulated entertainment only.

Offences

Enforcement is covered in chapter 11 however the key offences under this regime are:

- Carries out licensable activity without authorisation (S136).
- Knowingly allows licensable activity without authorisation (S136).
- Allows disorderly conduct on licensed premises (S140).
- Sale of alcohol to a person who is drunk (S141).
- Failure to leave licensed premises (S143).
- Sale of alcohol to children (S146).
- Allowing sale of alcohol to children (S147).
- Purchase of alcohol by children (S149).

4

The Gambling Act 2005

In 1999 the Government set up an independent review of gambling law by Sir Alan Budd. The Gambling Review Report "A Safe Bet for Success" was completed in 2001 and it made 176 recommendations under the following eight headings:

- A new legislative framework.
- Modern regulation for a modern industry.
- Benefits for consumers and business.
- The national lottery.
- Keeping crime out.
- Dealing with the downside.
- Joining up the policy.
- Implementing the changes.

The Government consulted on the report and published its response in March 2002 accepting the vast majority of the recommendations. In September 2003 a Parliamentary committee was set up to consider the draft Gambling Bill. The committee agreed with the overall framework of the Bill and made 139 recommendations and urged the Government to take a cautious approach.

The Government accepted most of these recommendations and the Bill was introduced into Parliament on 18 October 2004, receiving royal assent on 7 April 2005. The new law consolidates all gambling under one Act and the first Commencement Order came into force on 1st October 2005, which:

- Formally created the Gambling Commission (GC).

- Abolished the rule requiring customers to join casinos and bingo halls at least 24 hours before playing.
- Increased the number of jackpot machines allowed in a casino to 20.

The GA05 (S22) places a duty on the GC *"to permit gambling, in so far as the Commission thinks it reasonably consistent with pursuit of the licensing objectives".* Schedule 4 outlines provisions on the constitution and operation of the Commission which is responsible for granting operating and personal licences for commercial gambling operators and personnel working in the industry. The Commissions' other duties include:

- To draft a statement of principles (S23).
- To draft codes of practice for each sector (S24).
- To draft guidance for Local Authorities (S25).
- To advise Secretary of State on the incidence, manner, effects and regulation of gambling (S26).

The GC statement of principles state that in exercising its functions under the GA05 and in ensuring delivery of the licensing objectives, the GC will be guided by the following principles:

- It will regulate gambling in the public interest and it will do so vigorously.
- It will regulate in a transparent, accountable, proportionate, consistent and targeted manner.
- Its approach to regulation will be risk-based.
- Its assessment of risk will be led by the evidence, relevant information, and best regulatory practice in the light of international experience; where there is no evidence, it will take a cautious approach.
- It will consult widely.
- It will use its resources effectively.

The Minister responsible for gambling, Richard Caborn, said the GC was the start of a new era; *"The Gambling Commission will work to three key principles laid down in the Gambling Act - keeping out crime, protecting children and the vulnerable and ensuring gambling is fair. It will do so armed with new powers to investigate, prose-*

cute and levy unlimited fines. I'm confident that the Commission will be seen as a model for gambling regulation around the world in the years to come." The Commission's Chairman Peter Dean added that; *"The launch of the Gambling Commission is a major milestone in the most radical overhaul of gambling in half a century. The Gambling Act 2005 is significantly updating the laws governing gambling. It will be the Commission's job to make sure that those laws are obeyed, and that gambling in Britain is fair, safe and socially responsible".*

The overall principle of the GA05 is one of "Tri – Partite" control by:

- Government (DCMS).
- Gambling Commission.
- Licensing Authorities.

The GA05 (S1) states the licensing objectives as:

- Preventing gambling from being a source of crime or disorder, being associated with crime or disorder or being used to support crime.
- Ensuring that gambling is conducted in a fair and open way.
- Protecting children and other vulnerable persons from being harmed or exploited by gambling.

Licensing Authorities

The Licensing Authorities are defined in S2 as being:

- District Council in England.
- County Council in England where no District Council.
- County or County Borough Council in Wales.
- London Borough.
- Common Council of the City of London.
- Council of the Isles of Scilly.
- Licensing Boards in Scotland.

The GA05 (Part 8) places a duty on the Licensing Authority. Their main functions are to:

- Licence premises for gambling activity.
- Consider notices given for the temporary use of premises for gambling.
- Grant permits for gaming and gaming machines in clubs and miners' welfare institutes.
- Regulate gaming and gaming machines in alcohol licensed premises.
- Grant permits to family entertainment centres.
- Grant permits for prize gaming.
- Consider occasional use notices for betting at tracks.
- Register small societies' lotteries.

The GA05 (S349) requires Licensing Authorities to produce a policy in accordance with the Gambling Act 2005 (Licensing Authority Policy Statement) (England and Wales) Regulations 2006. Please refer to Chapter 2 for information on the development of policy.

Delegations

The function is delegated to the committee established under the Licensing Act 2003 with delegations allowed to the level shown in the table opposite.

Licences and Licensable Activities

The GA05 defines gambling as:

- Gaming - Playing a game of chance for a prize (S6).
- Betting - A transaction based on the outcome of a race, likelihood of event occurring or something true or not etc. (S9).
- Lottery - Pay to participate with prizes allocated based on chance (S14).

The GA05 will control gambling using registration, permits and the following three types of licence:

- Operating Licence (OL).
- Personal Licence.
- Premises Licence (PL).

Matter to be dealt with	Full Council	Sub-Committee	Officers
Licensing Policy	X		
No Casino Policy	X		
Fee Setting			X
Premises Application		Representations received and not withdrawn	No representations or withdrawn *
Variation Application		Representations received and not withdrawn	No representations or withdrawn *
Transfer Application		Representations from the GC	No representations from the GC
Provisional Application		Representations received and not withdrawn	No representations or withdrawn *
Review of PL		X	
Club gaming or machine permit		With objections	No objections
Cancellation of club gaming or machine permit		X	
Applications for other permits			X
Cancellation of permit			X
Temporary use notice (TUN)			X
Counter notice to a TUN		X	

X Lowest level of delegation
* Or if ALL parties agree

Exemptions from these classifications of gambling include spread betting (S10) controlled by the Financial Services & Markets Act 2000, the National Lottery (S15), equal chance gaming in licensed premises (S269/279) and free draws/games of skill (S14). Equal chance gaming will be permitted in premises with alcohol licences (on sales without a requirement to only serve alcohol with food) without requiring any specific permission, subject to statutory restrictions. These include limits on stakes and prizes, a prohibition on any levy or deductions from stakes and prizes, no charge to play, and a prohibition on linking games between premises. Such premises may also play bingo up to a threshold of £2,000 (either money taken or prizes awarded) in any seven day period.

For games of skill S14 requires the skill element to either deter a "significant proportion" from entering or eliminate a "significant proportion" of those who do. The GC have stated that they will not be setting a definitive figure for significant proportion and each case must be considered on its own merits, however many TV premium rate quiz shows may not meet this test.

Small lotteries, as defined in Schedule 11, are also exempt although some are subject to registration (please refer to permits and registrations below).

Private gaming and betting (Schedule 15) is not controlled by the GA05 if the gaming takes place in a domestic or residential setting with no access to the public and no charge to participate. Private betting is defined as "domestic" or "workers" betting.

The definitions include gambling which is delivered by "remote" means (S4), using:

- Internet.
- Telephone.
- Television.
- Radio.
- Any other electronic or other technology.

Operating Licence (OL)

An OL is issued by the GC under part 5 of the GA05 for the following ten categories (which may be combined). Any remote operations will need a separate licence:

- Casino operating licence.
- Bingo operating licence.
- General betting operating licence.
- Pool betting operating licence.
- Betting intermediary operating licence.

- Gaming machine general operating licence (adult gaming centre).
- Gaming machine general operating licence (family entertainment centre).
- Gaming machine technical operating licence.
- Gambling software operating licence.
- Lottery operating licence.

An OL is issued to a person, company or partnership, assessing the:

- Integrity of the applicant.
- Competence of the applicant.
- Financial circumstances of the applicant.

The application for an OL includes:

- Specification of the activities.
- Address in the UK.
- Whether convicted of a relevant offence.
- Whether convicted of any other offence.
- Fee.

The GA05 automatically attaches a number of conditions to an OL and S79 allows the GC to attach further conditions which may restrict:

- The nature of the licensed activities.
- The circumstances in which the licensed activities are carried on.
- The nature or circumstances of the licensee (or any other persons involved).

The GC has produced its Licence Conditions and Codes of Practice (November 2006) which includes the following sections for operating licences:

- Financial robustness.
- Protection of customer funds.
- Cash handling.
- Provision of credit and the use of credit cards.

- General provisions to allow fair and open gambling.
- Display of licence.
- Types and rules of casino and other games.
- Tipping of casino employees.
- Lotteries.
- Betting intermediaries.
- Pool betting.
- Access to premises.
- Requests for information.

Once granted an OL lasts indefinitely subject to:

- CG power to limit its operation (S111).
- Surrender (S113).
- Lapse (S114).
- Forfeiture (S115).
- Review (suspend or revoke) (S116).

Personal Licence

Personal licences are the responsibility of the GC under Part 6 of the GA05. A personal licence is required for anyone involved in specific management or operational functions (S127) and they fall into two categories:

- Personal Management Licences (PMLs).
- Personal Functional Licences (PFLs).

PMLs will be required for those holding the posts of:

- Managing director/CEO.
- Finance director.
- Compliance director.
- Marketing director.

PFLs are required for persons who (other than betting, lottery and arcade gaming):

- Influencing the outcome of gambling.

- Receiving or paying money in connection with gambling.
- Manufacture, install and maintain machines.

Applications must be made in a prescribed form and an individual may only hold one licence (S133). To ensure the crime prevention objective is achieved all personal licence holders are required to declare any relevant offences which are listed in Schedule 7. These include offences relating to:

- Gambling.
- Theft, robbery etc.
- False accounting.
- Blackmail.
- Handling stolen goods.
- Customs & excise.
- Violence.
- Sex offences.
- Drugs.
- Forgery and counterfeiting.
- SIA offences.

The following general conditions are attached to personal licences:

- Holder must take all reasonable steps to discharge their duties etc.
- Holder must keep up to date with legislation and codes etc.

Once granted a personal licence lasts indefinitely (S131), subject to:

- Surrender (S113).
- Lapse (S114).
- Forfeiture (S115).
- Revocation by the GC (S119).
- Disqualification (S136).

There is a duty to produce the licence when requested by a police officer or authorised enforcement officer (S134) and a duty to notify the Courts if convicted of a relevant offence (S109) and the GC (S138). The holder of an OL is also under a duty to inform the GC of any relevant offences by personal licence holders (S138).

Premises Licence (PL)

Premises licensing is the responsibility of the Licensing Authority under Part 8 of the GA05. A PL authorises the premises for one of five categories (S150):

- Casino.
- Bingo.
- Adult Gaming Centre (AGC).
- Family Entertainment Centre (FEC).
- Betting.

Only one category is allowed on a PL and only one licence per premises (S152) however the authorisation does allow specific gambling activities in addition to the primary activity. A Regional Casino PL and Large Casino PL authorises bingo, betting and an allocation of gaming machines. A Small Casino PL also authorises bingo and an allocation of gaming machines. In addition to the primary activity a Bingo PL and Betting PL both authorise an allocation of gaming machines (refer to Gaming Machines section below for allocation) and a Bingo PL allows prize gaming.

The GA05 imposes an initial limit on casinos and the Casino Advisory Panel, chaired by Professor Stephen Crow, recommended the location of the new casino licences (one regional, eight large and eight small) in January 2007, but this was rejected by the House of Lords in March 2007. At the time of writing it is not clear where these additional casinos will be located. Existing casinos have preserved rights and will not be affected by this restriction.

A premises applicant must hold (or have applied for) the appropriate OL and have the right to occupy the premises (S159). The application must be made in the prescribed manner including plans (S151), statutory notices (S160), fee (S184) and served on the following responsible authorities (S157):

- Local Authorities.
- The Gambling Commission.

- Police.
- Fire authority.
- Local planning authority.
- Environmental health.
- A body designated by the Licensing Authority as being competent to advise it on child protection issues, normally the local child safeguarding board.
- HM revenue and customs.
- Maritime and coastguard agency (where appropriate).
- British waterways board (where appropriate).

The statutory notices are designed to bring the application to the attention of any interested parties who are defined in the GA05 (S158) as *"Those living sufficiently close enough to the premises to be affected by the authorised activities, or a person representing them"* or *"Those with business interests that may be affected by the authorised activities, or a person representing them"*.

Plans

The plans must be drawn to scale and show:

- Boundary of the building stating the nature of adjoining premises.
- Entry and exit from the premises.
- Public toilets.
- Gambling areas.
- Gaming machines (Bingo and FEC).
- Other betting and alcohol (Tracks).

PL Determination

The Licensing Authority *"shall aim to permit the use of premises for gambling"* (S153) in accordance with:

- GC Codes of Practice.
- GC Guidance.
- Licensing objectives (subject to GC Codes and Guidance).

- Policy (subject to the above).

S153 sets a hierarchy of requirements which the Licensing Authority must follow. For instance the Licensing Authority could not grant an application which met the requirements of the licensing objectives and their policy but not the GC codes or guidance.

In determining whether to grant a PL a Licensing Authority may not have regard to the expected demand for the facilities which it is proposed to provide (S153) and S210 specifically excludes determining an application on the basis that planning regulations or building regulation approval has not been sought. However, this does not prohibit the Authority from taking into account extant planning permissions or building regulations.

There are three types of condition which may be attached to a PL:

- Mandatory (S167).
- Default (S168).
- Discretionary, set by the Licensing Authority (S169).

Mandatory and default conditions are prescribed in the GA05 (Mandatory & Default Conditions) (England & Wales) Regulations 2006 (referred to from now as the Conditions Regulations) for each premises type. Conditions attached by the Licensing Authority may not:

- Conflict with GC requirements (S169).
- Require membership (S170).
- Limit stakes or prizes (S171).
- Restrict machines numbers (S172).

The Conditions Regulations stipulate the mandatory and default conditions. Every PL will have the following conditions:

- The summary of the premises licence shall be displayed in a prominent place within the premises.
- The layout of the premises shall be maintained in accordance with the plan.

- The premises shall not be used for:
  - (a) The sale of tickets in a private or customer lottery, or
  - (b) The sale of tickets in any other lottery in respect of which the sale of tickets on the premises is otherwise prohibited

Depending on the premises type each PL will also be subject to the conditions relating to signage, position of ATM machines and access between premises as stipulated in the table below.

	Casino	Betting	Track	Bingo	AGC	FEC	Club	Pub	Other*
Casino		X	X	X	X	X	X[1.]	X[1.]	X
Betting	X		✓	X	X	X	X	X	X
Track	X	✓		✓	X	✓	✓	✓	✓
Bingo	X	X	✓		X	✓	✓	✓	✓
AGC	X	X	X	X		X	X[1.]	X[1.]	✓
FEC	X	X	✓	✓	X		✓	✓	✓
Club	X[1.]	X	✓	✓	X[1.]	✓		✓	✓
Pub	X[1.]	X	✓	✓	X[1.]	✓	✓		✓
Other*	X	X	✓	✓	✓	✓	✓	✓	

* Other commercial premises - restrictions apply.
1. With a GA05 permit.

Once granted a PL will normally last indefinitely (S191), subject to:

- Surrender (S192).
- Revocation for failure to pay annual charge (S193).
- Lapse (S194).
- Review (S197).

To provide a degree of certainty prior to development applicants are allowed to make a provisional application (S204) when:

- Premises are to be constructed.
- Premises are to be altered.
- Applicants expect to acquire premises.

For provisional applications there is no need for the applicant to hold an operating licence or have the right to occupy the premises. Full applications will be necessary prior to operation however and the Licensing Authority must disregard any comments made on full application which could have been addressed at the provisional stage (S205).

Premises shall not be used for gambling on Christmas Day (S183) and a PL may not be issued to a vehicle but may be issued to a passenger vessel or vessel situated at a fixed place (S211). A vehicle includes a train, aircraft, seaplane or amphibious vehicle (other than a hovercraft) and a vessel includes anything designed for use or situated on the water including a hovercraft.

Gaming Machines

The GA05 (S236) defines four categories of gaming machine A to D, which are sub divided by regulation, as follows:

A - which may accept any stake and pay unlimited prizes.
B1 - maximum stake of £2 and a maximum prize of £4,000.
B2 - maximum multiple stake of £100 and a maximum prize of £500.
B3 - maximum stake of £1 and a maximum prize of £500.
B4 - maximum stake of £1 and a maximum prize of £250.
C - maximum stake of £1 and a maximum prize of £35.
D - maximum stake of 10p (30p token) and a maximum prize of £5 (£8 non-money prize).

Only category D machines are playable by anyone under 18 and category A, B1 and B2 machines must allow for power interruption. Automated casino equipment and betting machines linked to live events are not classed as gaming machines.

A PL authorises the following number of gaming machines, in addition to the primary gambling activity (S172):

- Regional Casino – 1250, any category, subject to machine/table ratio.
- Large Casino – 150, category B C or D, subject to machine/table ratio.
- Small Casino – 80, category B, C or D, subject to machine/table ratio.
- Bingo – Four category B3/B4, any number of C or D.
- AGC – Four category B3/B4, any number of C or D.
- FEC – Any number of C or D.
- Betting – Four category B2 to D.

The GC has produced the Gaming Machine Technical Standards which cover the following topics:

Section 1: Hardware requirements.
Section 2: Software requirements.
Section 3: Critical memory requirements.
Section 4: Payment to the machine and to the game.
Section 5: Game requirements.
Section 6: Error requirements.
Section 7: Meter requirements.
Section 8: Display requirements.
Section 9: Progressive gaming devices in casinos.

Permits and Registrations

The GA05 continues with a permit/registration system for the following:

- FEC (with category D machines only).
- Pubs and clubs.
- Prize gaming.
- Small lotteries.

Such permits and registrations are the responsibility of the Licensing Authority.

An applicant for a permit must be a minimum of 18 years old and the Licensing Authority may only grant or refuse the permit. The Licensing Authority cannot attach conditions.

As previously covered a FEC may operate with any number of category C or D machines with an OL. If the premises only include category D machines then they may operate using a Schedule 10 permit.

Using a simple notification procedure (S282) premises licensed for the sale of alcohol (for consumption on the premises without any conditions requiring the sale of food) may operate up to two category C or D gaming machines. Pubs may apply for a permit allowing a greater number of category C or D machines (S283 & Schedule 13).

Clubs with a Club Premises Certificate may operate up to three gaming machines (B, C or D) and play bingo up to a threshold of £2,000 in any seven day period. A Licensing Authority can only refuse a club permit application on the following grounds:

- The applicant does not fulfil the requirements for a club (note that these are slightly different from the requirements to form a club under LA03).
- The applicant's premises are used mainly by children.
- An offence under the Act has been committed.
- A permit held by the applicant has been cancelled in the previous ten years, or
- An objection has been made by the GC or the police.

Premises with a CPC may use a fast-track approach which limits the Licensing Authority to rejecting on the following grounds only:

- The club is established primarily for gaming other than Schedule 12.
- The club provides facilities for other gaming.
- A permit held by the applicant has been cancelled in the previous ten years.

Prize gaming is defined in S288 as gaming in which the size of the prize is not determined by either:

- The number of persons playing or
- The amount paid.

Games such as bingo would fall into this category and they may be authorised by a permit from the Licensing Authority subject to limits set for:

- Participation fees.
- Prizes.

Operators of a lottery will require licences from both the GC and Licensing Authority however the GA05 exempts the following small lotteries:

- Incidental non-commercial lotteries. An incidental non-commercial lottery can only be staged in connection with an event, with no private gain, prescribed limits on costs and prizes, no rollover and tickets sold only during the event.
- Private lotteries. A private lottery is defined as a private society, work or residents lottery and must be run to either provide society funding or in the case of a work/residents lottery operated with no profit. There must be no rollover and there are restrictions on advertising.
- Customer lotteries. A customer lottery must operate at no profit with no rollover and restrictions on advertising and prizes (£50). There must be a minimum of seven days between lotteries.

A ticket in a private society lottery may only be sold or supplied by the promoter or another person who is a member of the same society, in a works lottery by the promoter or another person employed on the same premises, or in the case of a residents' lottery by the promoter or another person who resides on the same premises. Each ticket must state the name and address of the promoter or promoters of the lottery and the class of persons to whom the promoter(s) can sell or supply tickets. The price paid for each ticket in a private lottery must be the same, must be shown on the ticket and must be paid to the promoters of the lottery before any person is given a ticket. Rights conferred by tickets are not transferable and this should be made clear on the lottery tickets.

Certain lotteries that are seeking to raise funds are allowed if registered with the Licensing Authority, referred to as "small society lotteries". The society must be non-commercial i.e. established and conducted for charitable purposes or the purpose of enabling participation in, or of supporting, sport, athletics or a cultural activity for any other non-commercial purpose other than that of private gain. The registration restricts the lottery as follows:

- Promoted for the purpose of the society.
- Society receives a minimum 20% of the proceeds.
- Every ticket in the lottery must cost the same.
- Maximum proceeds £20,000 or £250,000 pa.
- Maximum prize £25,000 and rollover okay.
- Statement of dates, proceeds, costs etc.

All small society lottery tickets must:

- Identify the society.
- State the price (which must be the same for all tickets).
- State the name and address of the responsible member of the society, or external lottery manager.
- State the date of the draw.

The registration process will include:

- Prescribed forms.
- Purpose of society.
- Prescribed info.
- Fees (including annual charge).

Organisers must submit, within three months of the lottery, a return signed by a minimum of two authorised members including the following:

- The arrangements for the lottery (including the date on which tickets were available for sale or supply, the dates of any draw and the value of prizes, including any rollover).
- The proceeds.
- The amounts deducted by the promoters of the lottery in

providing prizes, including prizes in accordance with any rollovers.

- The amounts deducted by the promoters of the lottery in respect of costs incurred in organising the lottery.
- Any amount applied to a purpose for which the promoting society is conducted (at least 20% of the proceeds).
- Whether any expenses incurred in connection with the lottery were not paid for by deduction from the proceeds, and, if so, the amount of expenses and the sources from which they were paid.

The Licensing Authority must reject (S119) if the applicant has been refused (or revoked) an OL in the previous five years and may refuse to register an organisation on any of the following grounds:

- Not a non-commercial society.
- Relevant offences.
- Misleading or false information.

Temporary & Occasional Uses

A Temporary Use Notice (TUN) under Part 9 of the GA05 allows for the temporary use of premises under the following conditions:

- Applicant must hold an OL for the activity proposed.
- The premises are not used for gambling on more than 21 days in a 12 month period.

The notice must be served on the Licensing Authority a minimum of three months and one day before the proposed use of the premises and copied to the CG, police and revenue & customs. The notice must include:

- Details of the gambling activity.
- Address of the premises.
- Dates and times.
- Any previous similar use in the past 12 months.

Any of the consultees or the Licensing Authority itself may object to the use of the premises within 14 days and the Licensing Authority must hold a hearing when they can:

- Prevent the temporary use.
- Limit activities.
- Limit time periods.
- Attach conditions.

In addition the GA05 also allows the occasional use of tracks (which includes any sporting venues) for betting without the need for a premises licence using an Occasional Use Notice (OUN) under S39. The event and betting may be an ancillary use of land subject to a maximum of eight days in a "calendar" year. The notice must be served on the Licensing Authority and copied to the police and there is no provision for objections.

Children

Under the GA05 (S46) a person commits an offence if they invite, cause or permit a person under 18 to gamble.

The following premises must not allow access to children:

- Adult Gaming Centres.
- Betting.
- Casinos.

S45 defines a "child" as a person less than 16 years old and a "young person" as a someone between 16 and 18 years old with a "young person" also committing an offence if they:

- Gamble (S48).
- Enter restricted premises (S49).
- Provide facilities for gambling (S50).

Miscellaneous

The GA05 (S334) repeals the existing laws which voided betting contracts however the GC may deem a bet void using S336 if they determine it was unfair, namely if either party:

- Supplied insufficient, false or misleading information.
- Believed that a race etc was conducted in contravention of industry rules.
- Believed that an offence (or conviction) under S42 had been committed.

Offences

Enforcement is covered in chapter 11 however the key offences, in addition to those relating to children above are:

- Provision of facilities (S33).
- Use of premises (S37).
- Producing gambling software without an OL (S41).
- Cheating (S42).
- Chain gift schemes (S43).
- Make gaming machines available for use (S242).
- Manufacture or supply gaming machines (S243).
- Promote a non-exempt lottery (258)

5

Taxi Licensing

Unusually for matters covered in this book, the law relating to Hackney Carriages (HC) and Private Hire Vehicles (PHV) is different within and outside London. Within Greater London, responsibility for licensing and enforcement of HC and PHV lies with the Public Carriage Office (PCO), part of Transport for London (TfL) and under the control of the Mayor of London. Outside London, it is the responsibility of district, metropolitan and unitary Councils in England, and county and county borough Councils in Wales (all hereafter referred to as Councils).

The main narrative of this chapter will concentrate on the position outside Greater London with a brief overview of the differences and details of the London legislation at the end of the chapter. References in brackets are to *"Taxis – Licensing Law and Practice"* by James T H Button, 2nd Edition Tottel Publishing 2004.

Hackney Carriages and Private Hire Vehicles

There are fundamental distinctions between the two.

- HC, often referred to as taxis, and described as such in post 1985 legislation, are independent vehicles and can ply for hire, stand on a rank, can be hailed in the street and can be pre-booked.
- PHV lack the independence of HC and are tied to a private hire operator, through whom they must be pre-booked. They can not ply for hire, they can not stand in a rank, and they can not be hailed on the street.

Licensing Outside Greater London

The main legislation is contained in:

- Town Police Clauses Act 1847 (TPCA47).
- Town Police Clauses Act 1889 (TPCA89).
- Local Government (Miscellaneous Provisions) Act 1976 (LGMPA76).
- Transport Act 1980 (TA80).
- Transport Act 1985 (TA85).
- Disability Discrimination Act 1995 (DDA95).

The HC and PHV elements of this legislation apply across England and Wales with the exception of the LGMPA76. This must have been adopted by the Council which must be able to demonstrate that it has been adopted. According to the Department for Transport (DfT), all Councils in England and Wales have adopted the 1976 Act, except Plymouth City Council, which has its own similar legislation (for readers in Plymouth, most of the principles in the LGMPA76 are replicated in the City of Plymouth Act 1975, although section numbers will be different). For the purposes of this chapter, it is assumed that the LGMPA76 has been adopted.

In addition, in October 2006 the Department for Transport (DfT) issued its *"Taxi and Private Hire Vehicle Licensing: Best Practice Guidance"* which must be considered by Councils, although there is no statutory requirement to "have regard" to it.

The District Council

Licences are granted or refused, renewed or not, suspended or revoked and can be subjected to conditions by the Council (see Chapter 2 for details of the principles involved). There are rights of appeal (as of right, without any need to show merit) given to "persons aggrieved" against all those decisions (for further details on appeals, see Chapter 8)

Previous Convictions

One important factor which the Council will take into account when considering whether to grant, renew, revoke or suspend any licence is any previous criminal convictions recorded against the applicant or licensee. The Rehabilitation of Offenders Act 1974 (ROA74) allows certain convictions to be treated as "spent" after a period of time (dependent upon the original sentence not exceeding 2? years imprisonment) for most purposes. Until that point is reached, the conviction is "live". The period of time that must elapse before a conviction becomes spent can be extended if the person re-offends.

However, HC drivers and PH drivers are exempt from the provisions of the ROA74 by virtue of the ROA74 (Exemptions) Order 1975 (ROAEO75). This means that all previous convictions are "live" and can all be taken into account by the Council, and the Council can seek an enhanced check from the criminal records bureau. (see Button Chapter 5)

In respect of HC proprietor, PH operator and PHV applicants, these are not exempted by the ROAE75, but the Council can take spent previous convictions into account under the ruling in Adamson v Waveney District Council [1997] 2 All E.R. 898 QBD. In addition, events that have not lead to a conviction, but which may also have a bearing on the suitability of the person to be licensed can also be taken into account by the Council – see R v Maidstone Crown Court ex parte Olson [1992] COD 496 QBD and Leeds City Council v Hussain [2003] RTR 199 Admin Crt. (see Button Chapter 10).

The Council needs policies on how it will treat previous convictions and non-convictions in relation to drivers, vehicle licensees and PHOs. These will be different as a result of the different roles of various licensees.

Breach of Conditions

With the one exception of non-compliance with the requirement to comply with PH operator record keeping conditions (S56 LGMPA76), non-compliance with a condition attached to a HC or PH licence is not a criminal offence. Accordingly, the usual sanction for breach of conditions (whatever licence they may be attached to) is to bring the transgressor before the Council committee. (see Button Chapter 6).

They may then consider whether to take action, either suspension or revocation.

The powers to do so are contained in LGMPA76:

> S60 - HC and PHV licences.
> S61 - HC and PH drivers' licences.
> S62 - PH operators' licences.

HC Legislation: HC are governed principally by the provisions of TPCA47 (as amended), together with TPCA89, LGMPA76, and TA81 and TA85.

PHV Legislation: By contrast the legislation relating to PHV is reasonably straight forward to the extent that it is almost all in one place, which is the LGMPA76 with some references in the TA81 and TA85.

Licence Fees

There are two licence fee levying provisions in the LGMPA76, and in both cases, the fee is dependent on the grant of the licence. Although the fee can accompany the application, if the licence is not granted, the fee must be refunded. The one exception to that is the element of the fee that relates to the testing of vehicles. If the vehicle fails, the Council can still keep the costs of the test - see Kelly v Liverpool City Council [2003] 2 All ER 772 CA.

S53 LGMPA76 allows the costs of the issue and administration relating to drivers licences to be recovered via the licence fee. S70 LGMPA76 allows the costs of inspections of HC & PHV vehicles, provision of HC stands, administration costs in respect of vehicle inspections and stand provision, and control or supervision of HC & PHV can be recovered via the licence fees for vehicle and operators licences. (see Button Chapter 4).

HC Vehicles

A HC is defined in S38 of the TPCA47 as *"Every wheeled carriage, whatever may be its form or construction, used in standing or plying for hire in any street within the prescribed distance and every carriage standing upon any street within the prescribed distance, having thereon any numbered plate required by this or the special Act to be fixed upon a hackney carriage, or having thereon any plate resembling or intended to resemble any such plate as aforesaid, shall be deemed to be a hackney carriage within the meaning of this Act; and in all proceedings at law or otherwise the term "hackney carriage" shall be sufficient to describe any such carriage: . . .".* This definition is used in every piece of legislation since 1847. (see Button Chapters 8 & 9).

Any vehicle acting as a HC needs a HC proprietors' licence (S37 & S40 TCPA47), and any vehicle standing or plying for hire without a HC proprietors' licence commits an offence under S45 TPCA47. Once a HC proprietors' licence has been granted, the vehicle to which it applies is always a HC - see Hawkins v Edwards [1901] 2 KB 169 DC and must always be driven by a person who holds a HC drivers' licence issued by the same Council that licensed the HC S46 TPCA47.

A HC proprietors' licence allows the vehicle to ply or stand for hire throughout the district or zone, and that right cannot be limited by conditions attached to the HC proprietors' licence – see Maud v Castle Point Borough Council [2003] R.T.R. 7 CA. There are two exceptions:

- Private ranks at e.g. railway stations, airports and retail and leisure parks where access to the rank may be limited by permissions from the rank owner (although at railway station ranks, but no other private ranks, the other control provisions apply by virtue of S76 Public Health Act 1925); and,
- HC zones which exist in some districts as a result of local government reorganisations, in which case each zone is effectively a separate district for the purposes of HC licensing and use.

Conditions

Conditions that are "reasonably necessary" can be imposed by the Council on a HC proprietors' licence (S41 TPCA47; S47 LGMPA76).

Limiting HC Proprietors' Licences

The Council can limit the numbers of HC by refusing applications for HC proprietors licences over a specified number, but only if it *"is satisfied that there is no significant demand for the services of hackney carriages (within the area to which the licence would apply) which is unmet.".* (S37 TPCA47 as amended by S16 TA85). Such satisfaction can only come from an independent survey, ideally less that three years old – see R v Brighton Borough Council ex parte Bunch [1989] COD 558 DC.

If the Council is not so satisfied, it must grant any application, see e.g. Kelly & Smith v Wirral MBC (1996) 160 JP Rep 1047 CA and R (app Maud) v Castle Point Borough Council [2003] RTR 7 CA.

Although a Council can resolve to remove its numerical limit on HC proprietors' licences at any time, it must consult interested parties before such a course of action – see R v Great Yarmouth Borough Council ex parte Sawyer (1987) [1989] RTR 297n CA and Sardar v Watford Borough Council 30th June 2006 unreported Admin Crt.

Plying and Standing for Hire

Only HC can do this. As to whether a vehicle is standing or plying for hire is ultimately a question of fact. There are a considerable number of cases in this area but see in particular Nottingham City Council v Woodings [1994] RTR 72 DC followed by Chorley Borough Council v Thomas [2001] LLR 625 DC in relation to vehicles on public highways, and Young v Scampion 87 LGR 240 District Council, and Eastbourne Borough Council v Stirling [2001] RTR 65 DC in relation to vehicles on private land. The mere presence of a private vehicle (unlicensed) or a PHV (licensed) either alone or parked in company with other private vehicles or PHV does not in itself amount to plying or standing for hire.

A Council can use undercover officers by means of entrapment to prove unlawful plying for hire – see Nottingham City Council v Amin [2000] 2 All ER 946 DC, but any such officers should be authorised under the Regulation of Investigatory Powers Act 2000 (RIPA 2000) as Covert Human Intelligence Sources (CHIS). Although this is not the view of many District

Councils and police forces, in the absence of case law on the point it is an important and sensible precaution.

Ranks

HC stands or ranks can be created by byelaws made under S68 of TPCA47 (effectively obsolete as a creation method, although stands created by byelaws still have effect), or under S63 LGMPA76. The same LGMPA76 powers can be used to revoke or alter stands, and any stands created by byelaws are deemed to continue and have been made under this section. It is an offence for any vehicle other than a HC to park or wait on a stand (S64 LGMPA76).

Fares and Discounts

The Council can set fares for HC (PH operators are free to set their own for the PHV they operate), although a number of Councils do not do so, and allow negotiation between passenger and HC driver to establish a fare). Once set, the fare is simply the maximum that can be charged, and discounts can be offered, either on an individual basis, or generally by means of the meter being set at a lower rate than prescribed - see R v Liverpool City Council ex parte Curzon Ltd 1993 (Unreported) DC. It is an offence for a HC driver to charge more than the fare shown on the meter (S58 TPCA47).

There are theoretically three ways of setting HC fares, although the first two (a local Act incorporating TPCA47 and byelaws under TPCA47 are effectively obsolete) leaving S65 LGMPA76 as the widely used method.

Disability Discrimination Act 1995

Notwithstanding Part V of the DDA95, currently, there is no statutory requirement for HC or PHV to be capable of carrying disabled passengers. The Department for Transport announced in October 2003 that Taxi Accessibility Regulations will be introduced for certain "first phase" Councils from 2010 with all HC being wheelchair accessible by 2020 (subject to a possible exemption under Regulations made under S35 DDA95 if meeting the requirements would reduce the number of HC to an unacceptable level). See - www.publications.parliament.uk

Until then, and for all other areas, Councils are able to introduce wheelchair accessibility by conditions – see R v Manchester City Council ex parte Reid and

McHugh [1989] RTR 285 QBD.

Guide and assistance dogs must be carried in HC and PHV unless the driver has a medical exemption certificate – see the DDA95 (Taxis)(Carrying of Guide Dogs etc)(England and Wales) Regulations 2000 and S37 DDA95.

Under amendments to the DDA95 (introduced by the DDA05) all transport providers (including HC and PHVs) must not treat disabled people in a less favourable way than non disabled persons.

Suspension/Revocation (Proprietors)

A Council can suspend, revoke or refuse to renew a HC proprietors' licence on one of three grounds (S60 LGMPA76), namely:

- That the HC is unfit for use as a HC;
- That the HC proprietor has committed an offence or some other non-compliance with requirements of the TPCA47 or LGMPA76 Act; or
- Any other reasonable cause.

There are rights of appeal as outlined in Chapter 8, so the effect is delayed until either appeal period has expired, or any appeal is determined or abandoned.

Immediate suspension of a HC proprietors' licence can be effected by the Council by using S68 LGMPA76 on one of two grounds:

- That the HC is unfit for use as a HC, or
- That the taximeter (if fitted) is inaccurate

When S68 is used, there is no right of appeal, and only judicial review could be used to challenge the decision of the Council.

HC Drivers

Anyone who drives a HC must be the holder of a HC drivers' licence issued by the same Council that licensed the HC (S46 TPCA47). (see Button Chapter 10).

To be granted a HC Drivers' licence the applicant must:

- Be a fit and proper person to hold a HC Drivers' Licence (to the satisfaction of the Council); and
- Have held a full driving licence for at least 12 months at the date of application (not grant, which with delays in obtaining CRB checks etc can be considerably later);
  (S59 LGMPA76).

A full driving licence includes UK licences, Northern Ireland licences, EU licences and "exchangeable driving licences", and the requirement to hold it for one year is met even if the driver is disqualified provided they held it for one year before the disqualification - see R. v Crawley Borough Council Ex p. Crabb [1996] RTR 201 QBD.

In contrast to all other HC and PHV licences, conditions cannot be imposed on HC drivers licences – see Wathan v Neath Port Talbot County Borough Council (2002) All ER (D) DC. It should be noted that this is quite different from the PH drivers' licence where conditions can be imposed (S51 LGMPA76).

Drivers' Activity

The legislation imposes certain duties and requirements on HC driver. These include the following:

- There is a duty to take a hirer on any journey within the area of the Council (or zone) unless there is a "reasonable excuse" not to (S53 TPCA47);
- No agreement to pay more than the fare shown on the meter (if fitted) is enforceable, and any attempt to charge more is an offence (S55 & S58 TPCA47);
- The HC Driver cannot carry anyone other than the hirer, unless the hirer consents to their carriage (S59 TPCA47)
- The driver must produce his HC Drivers' Licence to a police constable or authorised officer of the Council on request (S53 LGMPA76).

Suspension/Revocation (Drivers)

A Council can suspend, revoke or refuse to renew a HC drivers' licence on one of three grounds (S61 LGMPA76), namely:

- That the driver has been convicted of an offence involving dishonesty;
- That the driver has been committed an offence under, or in some way not complied with the requirements of the TPCA47 or LGMPA76; or
- Any other reasonable cause.

There are rights of appeal as outlined in Chapter 8, so the effect is delayed until either the appeal period of 21 days has expired, or any appeal is determined or abandoned. S52 Road Safety Act 2006 has introduced the ability for the Council to suspend or revoke the licence with immediate effect if it is in the interests of public safety to do so.

Private Hire

PH licensing is wholly controlled by the LGMPA76. S80 contains the definitions including:

""Operate" means in the course of business to make provision for the invitation or acceptance of bookings for a PH vehicle;" and

""Private hire vehicle" means a motor vehicle constructed or adapted to seat fewer than nine passengers, other than a HC or public service vehicle or a London cab or tramcar, which is provided for hire with the services of a driver for the purpose of carrying passengers;"

PH Operators

Anyone who makes a provision for the invitation of bookings for a PHV must hold a PH operators' licence (S55 & S80 LGMPA76). (see Button Chapter 12).

An applicant for a PH operators' licence must be considered a "fit and proper person" before the Council can grant a PH operators' licence – S55 LGMPA76. Conditions that are "reasonably necessary" can be imposed on a PH operators' licence by the Council (S55 LGMPA76).

The licence must specify the address or addresses of the premises to be used by the PH operator, and if different premises are used without the licence being amended by the Council to reflect the change, then the operation is unlicensed – see Kingston upon Hull City Council v Wilson (1995) Times, 25 July DC.

All journeys by PHV must be booked via a PH operator who must maintain records of the booking in accordance with conditions attached to his PH opera-tors' licence and by the Act – see S56 LGMPA76. To discharge the booking, the PH operator must provide a PHV driven by a PH driver, and all three licences must have been issued by the same Council – see Dittah v Birmingham City Council, Choudry v Birmingham City Council [1993] RTR 356 DC. It is an offence under S46 LGMPA76 for a PH operator to knowingly use unlicensed drivers or vehicles.

An unlicensed vehicle provided by a PH operator at no charge constitutes operating – see St Albans District Council v Taylor [1991] The Times 30th May.

A PHV is not limited to working within the confines of the Council area in which it is licensed. A PH operator can advertise his service both within and outside the Licensing Authority area – see Windsor and Maidenhead RBC v Khan (trading as Top Cabs) [1994] RTR 87 DC. A PHV can be booked to pick up a fare anywhere, travel through any number of Council areas, and drop the fare anywhere - see Adur District Council v Fry [1995] 1 CLY 3148 DC.

The booking is deemed to be made with the PH operator who accepted it (S56 LGMPA76), but it can be subcontracted to another PH operator who must also be licensed by the same Council as the PH operator who originally accepted the booking – see North Tyneside MBC v Shanks [2001] All ER (D) 344 (Jun) QBD.

Vehicle Use Outside the PH Provisions of LGMPA76

It should be noted that an undertaking that takes telephone bookings for HC only (and no PHV) does not need a PH operator licence, and is outside the control of the LGMPA76 - see Brentwood Borough Council v Gladen 28th October 2004 unreported DC. HC used as PHVs (i.e. pre-booked) cannot charge more than the metered fare (if a meter is fitted) (S67 LGMPA76).

Weddings and Funerals

Vehicles (and their drivers) used in connection with weddings and funerals do not need to be licensed as PHV and PH drivers, and the person who arranges or books these does not need a PH operator (S75 LGMPA76).

"More than 7 days"

It was the case that a contract for the use of a specified vehicle for more than seven days, then the provider of that vehicle, vehicle and driver are outside the scope of the LGMPA76 - S75 – see Pitts v Lewis [1989] RTR 71n DC, Leeds City Council v Azam [1989] RTR 66 DC and Crawley Borough Council v Ovenden [1992] RTR 60 DC. This provision has been repealed by S53 Road Safety Act 2006 with a commencement date of January 2008, All "private hire" activity will need to be undertaken by licensed operators, vehicles and drivers, irrespective of the purpose of the journey, or any contractual arrangements that may be in place between the hirer and provider.

S265 Transport Act 2000

This inserted S79A to the Public Passenger Vehicle Act 1981. As a result, the use of a small bus (a vehicle which can carry up to eight passengers) carrying passengers not at separate fares is lawful without PH licences if it constitutes a "small part" of a large bus (vehicles which can carry more than eight passengers) PSV operators business.

Powers to Suspend, Revoke or Refuse to Renew an Operators Licence

A Council can suspend, revoke or refuse to renew a PH operators' licence on one of four grounds (S62 LGMPA76), namely:

- Any conduct on part of operator rendering him unfit to hold the licence.

- That the operator has committed an offence under, or in some way not complied with the requirements of the LGMPA76; or
- Any material change in the circumstances of the operator.
- Any other reasonable cause.

There are rights of appeal as outlined above, so the effect is delayed until either appeal period has expired, or any appeal is determined or abandoned.

PHVs

As with an HC, once a PHV licence has been issued, a PHV is always a PHV, and must therefore always be driven by a PH drivers - Benson v Boyce [1997] R.T.R. 226 DC and S46 LGMPA76 (see Button Chapter 13).

The Council cannot grant a PHV Licence unless the vehicle is (S48 LGMPA76):

- Suitable in type, size and design for use as a PHV;
- Not of such design and appearance as to lead any person to believe that the vehicle is a HC;
- In a suitable mechanical condition;
- Safe; and
- Comfortable

There must also be a suitable insurance policy in force before the licence can be issued - S48 LGMPA76. The Council cannot limit PHV numbers (S48 LGMPA76), nor insist on meters being fitted. If a meter is fitted voluntarily by the licensee, then it must work and passengers must be charged accordingly. However, it can be set to whatever rate the PH operator or PHV licence decides, as the Council cannot set fares for PHV (S71 LGMPA76).

Standards and Conditions

As with HC, the Council can determine minimum standards for PHVs, and then attach conditions to the licence to enforce those (S48 LGMPA76). Again, any conditions must be "reasonably necessary" and there are rights of appeal against the imposition of conditions, or the refusal to grant or renew a PHV Licence (S48 LGMPA76).

Stretched Limousines

If a stretched limousine is being used to transport passengers for hire, and it scats up to eight passengers, it is a PHV and must be licensed as such, and booked through a PH operator and driven by a PH drivers. Failure to comply with these requirements constitute an offence under S46 LGMPA76. If a vehicles has more than eight passenger seats it cannot be a PHV, and must be a PSV – see Vehicle and Operator Services Agency v Johnson 30th July 2003 Admin Crt unreported.

The Council may need to adopt different policies in relation to these vehicles.

PH Drivers

The requirements and control provisions for PH drivers are almost identical to HC driver, except the Council can impose conditions on PH drivers' licence under S51 LGMPA76. Again, such conditions must be reasonably necessary and rights of appeal against the imposition of any condition apply. (see Button Chapter 13)

HC and PH Licensing within Greater London

Greater London HC and PHV licensing is mainly contained in the following legislation:

- The London Hackney Carriages Act 1831 (LHCA31)
- The London Hackney Carriages Act 1843 (LHCA43)
- The London Hackney Carriage Act 1850 (LHCA50)
- The London Hackney Carriages Act 1853 (LHCA53)
- The London Hackney Carriage (No 2) Act 1853 (LHC(No2)A53)
- The Metropolitan Public Carriage Act 1869 (MPCA69)
- The London Cab Act 1896 (LCA96)
- The London Cab and Stage Carriage Act 1907 (LCSCA07)
- The London Cab Order 1934 (LCO34)
- The London Cab Act 1968 (LCA68)
- The London Cab Order 1972 (LCO72)
- The Transport Act 1985 (TA85)

- Private Hire Vehicles (London) Act 1998 (PHVLA98)
- Private Hire Vehicles (London) (Operators' Licences) Regulations 2000
- Private Hire Vehicles (London) (London PHV Driver's Licences) Regulations 2003
- Private Hire Vehicles (London) (London PHV Licences) Regulations 2004

As mentioned above, generally the concepts relating to HC and PHV licensing outside Greater London apply within Greater London. The administration and enforcement lies with Transport for London (TfL) acting via the Public Carriage Office (PCO), not the London Borough Councils, but the principles are similar. However, there are some differences, and of course, the legislative references are different. Outlined below are the principle differences, and references to provisions, following the same layout as the outside Greater London narrative.

London HC Vehicles

A London HC is defined in S4 MPCA69 as:

'"Hackney carriage" shall mean any carriage for the conveyance of passengers which plies for hire within the limits of this Act, and is neither a stage carriage nor a tramcar.' (For further details on London HC vehicles generally see Button Chapters 8 and 9).

The limit of the Act is Greater London – see S2 MPCA69 and S76 London Government Act 1963, S323 as amended by the Greater London Authority Act 1999.

The PCO can grant London HC licences – S6 MPCA69 and LCO34.

Although there is no case establishing whether a London HC is always a London HC and must therefore be driven by a licensed driver, PCO have taken the view that this is not the case, and when the vehicle is not working, it can be driven by people who do not hold a London HC drivers licence.

A London HC can be used anywhere within Greater London, although certain drivers are restricted to suburban areas (Art 27 LCO34).

A London HC licence is not subject to conditions as such, but conformity with the conditions of fitness (made under Art 7 LCO34) and LCO34 is required.

TfL/PCO cannot impose a limit on the number of London HC licences it grants.

Plying and standing for hire is the same as outside Greater London.

London HC Stands are created under S4 LHCA50.

Fares are set by TfL/PCO under S1 LCSCA07 and Arts 40 & 41 LCO34. The fare must be charged and no discounts can be offered (Arts 40 & 41 LCO34).

The DDA95 applies within Greater London, and all London HCs are wheelchair accessible.

Suspension or revocation of a London HC is governed by Art 19 LCO34.

London HC Drivers

This is very similar to the position outside London. (For further details on London HC drivers generally see Button Chapter 10).

The power to grant is contained in S8 LHCA43 and the requirement for a London HC drivers licence is found in S8 MPCA69. The criteria for grant are in Art 25 LCO34.

The responsibilities and duties imposed on London HC drivers are very similar to those outside Greater London.

A London HC drivers licence can be suspended or revoked under Art 30 LCO34.

PH in Greater London

PH Licensing in Greater London is relatively new, being introduced by PHVLA98. Again, it is administered by TfL/PCO. Generally, the London legislation is based on the LGMPA76. The differences from the position outside Greater London are minor and if further information is required, the reader is referred to Button.

Offences

Enforcement is covered in chapter 11 however the key offences under this regime are:

- Unlawful plying for hire by a vehicle not licensed as a HC within the district or zone (S45 TPCA47).
- Licensed HC being driven by unlicensed driver (S47 TPCA47).
- Charging more than the metered fare in a HC (S55 TPCA47).
- Using an unlicensed vehicle as a private hire vehicle (S46 LGMPA76).
- Licensed PHV being driven by unlicensed driver (S46 LGMPA76).
- Operating a PHV without a PH operators licence (S46 LGMPA76).
- Operating an unlicensed vehicle as a PHV (S46 LGMPA76).
- Operating a licensed PHV when the driver is not licensed as a PH driver (S46 LGMPA76).

6

Animal Licensing

This chapter covers the following licensing regimes:

- Animal boarding.
- Dangerous wild animals.
- Dog breeders.
- Performing animals.
- Pet shops.
- Riding establishments.
- Zoos.
- Animal Welfare Act.

A wide range of statutory controls exist to protect animals through a framework of licences, registrations and permits that concern:

- Animal welfare and prevention of cruelty.
- The eradication and prevention of diseases in animals.
- Animal movements (including importation and exportation).
- Treatment and slaughter.
- Animal experimentation and pest control.
- Preserving endangered species and wildlife conservation.

The legislation gives wide powers to the Department for Environment, Transport and the Regions (DEFRA), usually enforced through ministerial veterinary practitioners, and to local authorities. This chapter focuses on premises-based licensing. These are normally businesses operated for commercial gain however it includes an individual who kept exotic animals controlled by the Dangerous Wild

Animals Act 1976 (DWA76).

Licensing control of animal establishments is not uniform however there are common features and exceptions (refer to table).

Common Features	Examples of 'exceptions to the rule'
Licences are granted specific to the person and the premises.	For dog breeders, account is taken of bitches housed elsewhere.
Generally there is no mechanism to vary or transfer a licence.	The local authority can unilaterally vary DWA licences at any time.
Annual licences with a common expiry date of 31st December.	A Zoo licence is granted for a period of six years.
Conditions can be attached to licences.	Cannot be attached to registrations for performing animals.
The grant of a licence does not confer any rights in respect of a licence of another type.	A pet shop owner can keep dangerous wild animals without the need for a DWA licence.
No time limit for a local authority to determine an application.	Dog Breeding Establishment licence must be determined within three months.
There is no mechanism for the grant of provisional licences.	Riding Establishments can be granted a three-month licence.
Invertebrates and usually excluded from the definition of 'animals'.	Insect species come with the scope of Zoo licensing.

Unlike the LA03 and GA05, animal licensing legislation does not expressly set out objectives, however the primary purpose is generally accepted as securing minimum standards for the health and welfare of animals. Certain licences include references to matters other than the health and welfare of the animals alone, predominantly public protection and preventing nuisance. Two obvious examples are requiring that insurance policies be held to compensate people who could be injured by escaping dangerous wild animals and ensuring that animal enclosures in zoos are designed to protect visitors.

Each statute contains a provision allowing the local authority to charge a fee, which is normally demanded at the time of application. No direction is given on whether the local authority is bound to refund the licence fee (or part of it) if, for instance, the application is either refused or withdrawn. Separate fees cannot be levied for variations or transfers.

Animal Boarding

Commercial boarding of cats and dogs must be licensed under the Animal Boarding Establishments Act 1963 (ABEA63). There is no requirement for the licensing of premises that look after other pet animals.

Animal boarding establishments are defined in S5 as the carrying on at any premises (including a private dwelling) of a business of providing accommodation for other people's cats and dogs. This will include a home boarding service where pets are cared for in a person's own home for payment. Whilst boarding establishments tend to specialise in either cats or dogs it would be possible to authorise the keeping of both animal types on the same site by the grant of a single ABE licence.

The main activity of the premises is important because if animal boarding is ancillary to another animal-related purpose then no licence is required i.e. if the boarding occurs at a veterinary practice or dog-training establishment. Similarly no licence is required where the dogs or cats are housed because of a requirement of 'diseases of animals' legislation, such as a quarantine facility.

The ABEA63 covers *"a business of providing accommodation for other people's animals"*. Therefore a licence would not be required where a relative or friend cares for the animal while the owner was away on holiday. Animal sanctuaries, sometimes called "refuges" or "re-homing centres" usually fall outside regulatory control as they are charitable concerns and not businesses and "dog walking" and "dog sitting" services are not licensable as the sitter does not provide accommodation.

Under S1 before granting a licence a Licensing Authority will need to be satisfied that the dogs and/or cats will be suitably fed, accommodated, exercised and protected from disease and fire.

Licensing Authorities are able to set their own conditions and most have adopted (wholly or in part) the model licence conditions issued in October 1995 by the Chartered Institute of Environmental Health (CIEH) which cover the following:

- Display of licence.
- Construction of kennels/cattery.

- Numbers of animals.
- Premises management.

The licence is specific to the person and the premises but there is an allowance for the short-term extension of a licence for the purpose of winding-up a deceased licence-holder's estate.

S1 requires that a register has to be kept to record the dates of arrival and departure and their owner's names and addresses. The register must be available for inspection.

Dangerous Wild Animals

Concerns about public safety by the keeping of dangerous species in the community led to the Dangerous Wild Animals Act 1976 (DWA76). The purpose of the DWA76 is to prevent harm to humans from escaping animals but it also provides important measures of protection for the captive animals. Certain animal welfare organisations such as the RSPCA are against the keeping of exotic animals as pets as a matter of principle but a local authority must judge each application on its merits and consider the grant of a licence where it believes that all conditions can be satisfactorily met.

The provisions prohibit the keeping of the scheduled species of animal except in accordance with a licence from the Local Authority (S1). Exceptions exist for zoos, circuses (including their winter quarters), pet shops and establishments registered for performing animal experiments (under the Animals [Scientific Procedures] Act 1986). No exemption exists merely because of the fact that the dangerous wild animal is immature and therefore not a threat. Therefore a "joey" will need to be included on a licence in addition to its kangaroo mother.

"Keeping" of a dangerous wild animal means having the animal in one's "possession". When the animal cannot be identified to be in the possession of anybody, it is treated as being in the possession of the person who last had possession of it. However, a person is not treated as a "keeper" if he is only holding the animal to prevent it from causing damage (including injuries); for it to undergo veterinary treatment; or transporting it on behalf of another.

The DWA76 only regulates the keeping of certain species of animal that are set out in Schedule (last amended by the DWA Act 1976 [Modification] Order 1984). The list giving both the scientific and common names is largely made up of exotic species that are not indigenous to the British Isles. It cannot be assumed that all animals that are liable to cause harm appear on the list, for example large constrictor snakes do not. The schedule includes:

Examples of DWA	
Mammals	Common Names
Marsupials	Kangaroos, Tasmanian Devils
Primates	Monkeys, Tamarins, Lemurs, Apes
Edentates	Sloths, Anteaters
Rodents	Porcupines, Capybara
Carnivores	Pandas, Wolves, Big Cats, Badgers, Hyenas, Bears
Pinnipedes	Walrus, Seals, Sealions
Elephants	Elephants
Odd-Toed Ungulates	Horses, zebras, Rhinos, Tapirs
Hydraxes	Hydraxes (Dassies)
Aardvark	Aardvark
Even-toed Ungulates	Antelopes, Buffalo, Camels, Llama, Giraffe, Hippos
Birds	
Emu & Ostrich	Emus, Ostriches
Reptiles	
Crocodilians	Alligators, Caimans, Crocodiles, Gharial
Lizards & Snakes	Venomous Snakes, Vipers, Cobras, Rattlesnakes.
Invertebrates	
Spiders & Scorpions	Venomous Spiders, Buthid Scorpions

A Local Authority receiving a valid application must be satisfied that:

- It is not contrary to the public interest on grounds of safety or nuisance.
- The applicant for the licence is a suitable person to hold it.
- The animal's accommodation is escape-proof and suitable as regards construction, size, temperature, lighting, ventilation, drainage, cleanliness and the number of animals that can be suitably accommodated.
- The animal will be supplied with adequate and suitable food, drink and bedding materials and be visited at suitable intervals.
- The animal will be protected in case of fire or other emergency.
- All reasonable precautions will be taken to prevent and control the spread of infectious diseases and

- The animal can take adequate exercise within its accommodation.

The application for a licence is prescriptive. It must:

- Specify the species of animal and the number of animals of each species proposed to be kept.
- Specify the premises where any animal concerned will normally be held (which must be within the local authority's area).
- Be made by a person who is neither under 18 years old nor disqualified from keeping any dangerous wild animal.
- Be accompanied by such fee as the authority may stipulate.

The applicant must establish himself as the person who both owns and possesses the dangerous wild animal, or who proposes both to own and possess it. A common condition on a pet shop licence is for dangerous wild animals not to be released until a valid DWA licence is shown to the proprietor.

Similar to the situation with riding establishments, local authorities must consider a report by a vet before determining a DWA licence application (S1). The report will assess the suitability of the arrangements at the premises where the animal will normally be held. Whist the DWA76 does not stipulate it, Councils will often seek the advice of an experienced vet who specialises in the particular animal species.

If the Council considers the premises suitable, it may grant a licence subject both to mandatory conditions detailed in the DWA76 and any other discretionary condition which cover the following:

- The animal to be kept by no person(s) other than those named on the licence.
- The premises where the animal is normally held to be specified on the licence.
- The animal not to be moved from the premises except in the circumstances specified in the licence.
- Holding of a current insurance policy to cover any damage caused by the animal.
- Restricting the numbers and types of DWA to be kept under the licence.

- The licence-holder to make a copy available at all reasonable times to any person entitled to keep any animal under the authority of the licence.
- Other conditions to secure the objectives considered when determining the licence (as explained above), such as security measures and the suitability of the animal's accommodation.

The Council can vary or revoke a DWA licence and prosecute for breaches of licence conditions. This includes offences committed by a person who although not a licence holder is entitled to keep the animal under the authority of the licence. The Licensing Authority may seize the DWA and keep the animal, destroy it or otherwise dispose of it without having to compensate the owner and may recover its costs from these parties.

Courts can cancel licences when convictions under the DWA76 are secured. Courts can also disqualify individuals from keeping dangerous wild animals because of such convictions and other offences under certain other animal protection laws.

It is an offence to obstruct vets, Council officers and others who have been authorised under the DWA76. However, there is no power to enter under warrant where an animal is suspected of being kept without a licence.

The fee required to accompany the application is not dependent on the grant of the licence. The level of fee should be sufficient to meet the direct and indirect costs the Council is likely to incur. This will encompass the costs of inspections by both the Council's vet and its own officers.

Dog Breeders

The Breeding of Dogs Act 1973 (BDA73), requires keepers of dog breeding establishments to obtain a licence from their Local Authority. The definition of a breeding establishment, and indeed the whole licensing system, was significantly changed by the Breeding and Sale of Dogs (Welfare) Act 1999. Home Office Circular 53/1999 contained guidance to Local Authorities to assist them in interpreting the 1999 Act.

A person keeps a breeding establishment for dogs at any premises if he or she carries on at those premises a business of breeding dogs for sale. The commercial element is a crucial factor; anyone carrying on a dog breeding business will normally need to be licensed regardless of the number of litters involved. However, S4 introduced a presumptive test. This provides that anyone who produces five or more litters in any period of 12 months will need a licence. In such a case the local authority does not need to prove that the person is carrying on a business of breeding and selling dogs. The bitches producing the litters can be kept elsewhere on the breeder's behalf by any number of other people.

It is often difficult to prove whether or not someone is pursuing a business enterprise. It is for the local authority to decide on the facts of each case. "Hobby breeders" who are not motivated by profit will not fall within this definition of a licensed breeder, even if they occasionally sell some puppies to cover their expenses.

Local Authorities have the discretion to grant licences unless the applicant is disqualified under certain specified statutes. In deciding whether to grant a licence for the first time, the Council must arrange for the premises to be inspected jointly by a vet and an officer of the authority. Renewal applications can be made by a vet or an authorised officer, or both. A report assessing the applicant, the premises and any other relevant matter must be considered before determining the application (S1). The Local Authority must have regard for the need for securing:

- That the dogs will at all times be kept in accommodation suitable as respects construction, size of quarters, number of occupants, exercising facilities, temperature, lighting, ventilation and cleanliness.
- That the dogs will be adequate supplied with suitable food, drink and bedding material, adequately exercised, and visited at suitable intervals.
- That all reasonable precautions will be taken to prevent and control the spread among the dogs of infectious or contagious diseases.
- That appropriate steps will be taken for the protection of dogs in case of fire or other emergency.
- That all appropriate steps will be taken to secure that the dogs

will be provided with suitable food, drink, and bedding material and adequately exercised when being transported to or from the breeding establishment.

- That bitches are not mated if they are less than one year old.
- That bitches do not give birth to more than six litters of puppies each.
- That bitches do not give birth to puppies before the end of the period of twelve months beginning on the day on which they last gave birth to puppies.
- That accurate records in a prescribed form are kept at the premises and made available for inspection.

Conditions can be attached to the granted licence in order to secure all these objects.

The form of record to be kept by licensed dog breeders for each breeding bitch was introduced in the Breeding of Dogs (Licensing Records) Regulations 1999. In the regulations made under the BSDAWA99, the Sale of Dogs (Identification Tag) Regulations 1999 specified the information required to be displayed on a dog's identifying tag or badge.

Statutory rights of entry exist for appointed vets and authorised officers who have the right to enter at all reasonable times:

- To inspect the premises.
- To inspect animals on the premises.
- To ascertain whether any offence has been or is being committed on the premises.

It is an offence to obstruct or delay any person exercising their powers of entry or inspection and keeping a dog breeding establishment without a licence and contravening a licence condition are both offences under the BDA73.

Where a person is convicted, a court has the power to cancel his licence and disqualify him from keeping a dog breeding establishment and/or any dog of whatever description. A further order can be made to require the offender to surrender a dog in his possession to a specified person and pay for its care until permanent arrangements are made for its care or disposal.

Performing Animals

The Performing Animals (Regulation) Act 1925 (PARA25) is of particular relevance to circuses and others working with animals in the entertainment industry. It requires anyone who trains or exhibits animals to register with their Local Authority, declaring details of their animals.

Unlike the other regimes covered in this chapter, the Local Authorities for the purposes of this legislation are County, Unitary, Metropolitan district and London Borough Councils, and the Common Council for the City of London.

It is important to note that the PARA25 creates a system of registration and, unlike the other regimes, not a licensing duty. This inevitably results in a loose system of control with significant defects from the point of view of enforcers and animal rights campaigners. Despite its limitations, it nevertheless is valuable in that it offers Local Authority and police officers powers to enter circuses at all reasonable times to check on how animals are being treated and housed (S3). This becomes important because circuses are exempt from both the Zoo Licensing Act 1981 and the Dangerous Wild Animals Act 1976. Officers are empowered to require certificates of registration to be produced but they cannot get on or behind a stage during a performance.

The term "exhibit" has wide scope and means exhibiting an animal at any entertainment to which the public are admitted, whether on payment or otherwise, unless the animals being exhibited for bona fide purposes (S5). There is no need to register for the training or exhibition of animals for military, police, and agricultural or sporting purposes.

Schedule 1 to the PARA25 sets out a prescribed form for registration applications. Applicants for registration must contain particulars of the animals and the general nature of the performances in which they are to be used. Schedule 2 specifies the form of register; Schedule 3 the Certificate of Registration; and Schedule 4 the form for applying to vary the particulars entered in the register.

The applicant must give an outline of what is done by the animals taking part in the performance, should state the approximate duration and frequency of performances and the number of animals taking part.

Importantly, the Local Authority cannot refuse a certificate of registration unless that individual is prohibited from exhibiting or training a wild animal or disqualified from being registered by order of a court. A copy of each certificate of registration issued must be transmitted by the Local Authority to the Secretary of State (S1).

An application for registration must be accompanied by the payment of *"such fee as appears to the local authority to be appropriate"*. A charge can also be made for inspecting or taking copies of the official register.

Each registration can include an unlimited number of animals and may include animals they hope to acquire. There is no requirement to cancel or update an original register entry: and since it is a system of registration and not licensing, there is no duty to renew registration certificates.

Animal trainers and exhibitors need not show any qualifications or relevant experience to become registered. Furthermore, there are no guidelines on acceptable standards of welfare or other criteria against which an inspection can be made. For example, there are no stipulations on the maximum permitted time that an animal can train or perform.

Prohibition under S2 of PARA25 can follow a complaint made to a Magistrates' court by a police or Council officer who believes that an incident of cruelty to a performing animal has occurred. In making an order the Court can alternatively impose conditions on the training or exhibition of animals. Any order only takes effect after seven days, which is the period allowed for appeal to the Crown court. Orders are suspended until an appeal is determined, otherwise the particulars of the prohibition or restriction is endorsed on the issued certificate and entered on the Council's register.

Pet Shops

The commercial sale of companion animals is governed by the Pet Animals Act 1951 (PAA51), as amended by the Pet Animals Act 1951 (Amendment) Act 1983. A pet shop is defined in S7 of PAA51 as premises of any nature (including a private dwelling of a business) for selling animals as pets and includes the keeping of animals in any such premises with a view to their being sold in the course of such a business, whether by their keeper or any other persons.

"Animals" in this context include those kept for ornamental purposes so the sale of Koi carp from garden centres, which has become very popular in recent years, will be licensable. On the other hand, the PAA51 only covers vertebrates, so the trade in insects such as tarantulas and other arachnids does not need licensing.

For the definition of "keeping a pet shop", a key factor is that pet sales take place as a part of a "business enterprise". The occasional sale is permitted for instance, of "surplus" puppies from litters. These might be either the unwanted offspring produced by a family pet or the by-product of a breeding programme by a hobbyist who shows pedigree dogs.

The obligation to obtain a licence is confined to the "selling of animals" as pets, for cats and dogs the law defines this will include "selling wholly or mainly for domestic purposes", therefore the sale of guard dogs or other working dogs is excluded.

A licence under the PAA51 will allow dangerous wild animals on premises without the need for a DWA76 licence. Some animal welfare organisations such as the RSPCA generally discourage this practice and, indeed, the sale of all exotic species. This is mainly because the prospective purchasers of these animals can be unfamiliar with the animal's behaviour, needs and suitability as a pet.

S2 states that it is an offence to carry on a business of selling animals as pets in any part of a street or public place, or at a stall or barrow in a market. Opinions vary on the interpretation of what constitutes a "public place". Some authorities have licensed temporary sales and auctions where commercial pet sales take place on a variety of sites not ordinarily used for that purpose; and where the pet sales are ancillary to another activity, such as demonstrations, exhibitions and shows. Examples have variously included reptile fairs in village halls; bird auctions at exhibition centres; and koi carp sales at agricultural shows.

The CIEH issued a circular in July 2001 stating that it would be ultra vires to grant a licence for a "pet fair". The CIEH later qualified its advice to clarify that it continues to be legitimate for sales of pet animals to go on by, and between, animal enthusiasts at club or society meetings, where the transactions do not form part of business dealings.

The PAA51 bans pet shops from selling animals to anyone where there is reasonable cause to believe they are under the age of 12 (S3).

Application forms for new pet shop licences will usually ask applicants to declare whether they are disqualified from having a licence. This is to reveal any disqualification following a prosecution under the PAA51 or other preceding Acts which provide protection to animals. Courts can also revoke a pet shop licence following conviction.

The Licensing Authority will assess the suitability of the applicant as well as his premises. This is partly to ensure that there is sufficient technical expertise and knowledge to comply with all the licence conditions. Unless an applicant can show sufficient relevant experience he will normally have to be qualified, or have employed someone on his staff who has such a qualification, usually the City and Guilds Certificate in Pet Shop Management.

Local Authorities must have regard to the need for securing (S1):

- Suitable accommodation in terms of size, temperature, lighting, ventilation and cleanliness.
- Adequate supplies of food and drink and that visits are made at suitable intervals.
- That immature mammals (but not other species) are not sold at too early an age.
- The prevention among animals of infectious diseases.
- Appropriate steps in case of fire or other emergency.

The Local Government Association's Model Standards for Pet Shop Licence Conditions were last revised in November 1998. In addition to standard conditions, Councils may attach conditions relating to specific species such as the numbers that can be held in stock and the density of cages, hutches, tanks etc.

Riding Establishments

Two statutes govern the licensing scheme for riding establishments. The principal Act, the Riding Establishments Act 1964 (REA64), was significantly amended by the 1970 Act of the same name (REA70). The REA64 forbids the keeping of a riding establishment except under the authority of a licence issued by the Local Authority (S1). Certain exceptions exist, for instance where the business is carried on at defence establishments or where the horses are kept solely for police purposes (S6).

The two primary purposes of licensing are to prevent animal suffering and to prevent injuries to riders.

The term "riding establishment" means the *"carrying on of a business of keeping horses to let them out on hire for riding, or for use in providing instruction in riding for payment, or both"*. A licence is therefore not required if no instruction is being given or if the horse is not actually let out on hire (S6). The place at which the riding establishment is run is taken as the place at which the horses are kept. Horse includes *"any mare, gelding, pony, foal, colt, filly or stallion and also any ass, mule or jennet"*.

A licence may be granted annually by application of an individual over the age of 18 years or a body corporate. The payment of a fee determined by the Council must accompany the application.

Upon receipt of an application the Council will commission an inspection report from a specialist vet. (The Royal College of Veterinary Surgeons keeps a register of members of the Panel of Approved Riding Inspectors.) The report will consider the suitability of the premises for keeping a riding establishment and describe the condition of the premises and the horses on it. If the management of the establishment is to be entrusted to another person by the applicant, the suitability and experience of the manager must also be assessed and reported upon.

Persons disqualified under the Act or legislation for the protection of animals cannot be given a licence (S1). In deciding whether or not to grant a licence, or provisional licence, the Council must, without prejudice to its right to refuse a licence on other grounds, have regard to the following matters:

- That the applicant and/or manager is suitable and qualified.
- The health, condition and fitness of the horses, which must be suitable for the purpose.
- That the feet of all animals are properly trimmed and that, if

shod, their shoes are properly fitted and in good condition.

- The accommodation for horses is suitable as respects construction, size, number of occupants, lighting, ventilation, drainage and cleanliness.
- There is adequate pasture (if horses are maintained at grass), shelter and water and that supplementary feeds will be provided as and when required.
- There are adequate supplies of suitable food, drink, bedding materials, and horses to be adequately exercised, groomed and rested and visited at suitable intervals.
- Reasonable precautions are in place to prevent and control the spread of disease among the horses and to provide veterinary first-aid equipment and medicines.
- Arrangements exist for the protection and extrication of horses in case of fire.
- There is adequate accommodation for forage, bedding, stable equipment and saddlery.

For the assessment of the applicant/manager an "Approved Certificate" means any one of the following certificates issued by the British Horse Society, namely:

- Assistant Instructor's Certificate, Instructor's Certificate and Fellowship.
- Fellowship of the Institute of Horse.
- Any other Certificate for the time being prescribed by order of the Secretary of State.

Full licences can continue for one year beginning on the day on which they came into force and then expire. The date of operation, depending upon the wishes of the applicant, is either the day on which it is granted or the 1st January next.

The REA70 introduced provisional licences. These can operate for three months from the day on which they are granted and are used where the local authority is satisfied that it would not be justified in issuing a full licence. The three months' period of operation may be extended for a further period of not exceeding three months.

On the death of a licence holder, the licence passes to his personal representative for a period of three months and then expires. The three-month period may be extended at the Councils' discretion.

On granting a licence the Council will specify conditions which are necessary or expedient in order to achieve the objectives set out in matters for consideration explained above (S1). In addition, the following rules are required to be followed, whether specified in the licence or not:

- A horse found on inspection of the premises by an authorised officer to be in need of veterinary attention cannot be returned to work until a veterinary certificate is obtained.
- No horse will be let out on hire for riding or used for providing instruction in riding without supervision by a responsible person of the age of 16 years of over unless (in the case of a horse let out for hire for riding) the holder of the licence is satisfied that the hirer of the horse is competent to ride without supervision.
- The carrying on of the business of a riding establishment shall at no time be left in the charge of any person under 16 years of age.
- The licence holder must hold a current public liability insurance policy to provide an indemnity against liability to pay damages for accidental injuries or property damages arising from the activities.
- A register shall be kept by the licence holder of all horses in his possession aged three years and under and usually kept on the premises, which shall be available for inspection by an authorised officer at all reasonable times.

Possible offences are listed in the amended 1964 Act (S1, S2 and S3). It is an offence to operate an establishment without a licence, or to be in breach of a licence condition, or to obstruct an authorised inspector. Other offences relate to the care and treatment of horses used in the business.

Zoos

The licensing of zoos is a complex subject requiring the input of specialist personnel and the thorough understanding by all involved of the standards of care demanded for a wide range of animal species. For this reason, whilst Local Authorities are responsible for licensing zoos located wholly or mainly in their area, they are supported by DEFRA who have issued comprehensive guidance in the form of ministerial codes and circulars and maintain a list of zoo inspectors. Typically inspection teams will be made up of two of these inspectors nominated by the Secretary of State and up to three appointed by the Local Authority, at least one of whom must be a veterinary surgeon or practitioner.

Animals covered by the Zoo Licensing Act 1981 (ZLA81) are of the classes of Mammalia, Aves, Reptilia, Amphibia, Pisces and Insecta and any other multi-cellular organism that is not a plant or fungus (S21). A zoo is an establishment where such wild animals (not normally domesticated in Great Britain) are kept for display (S1). Public exhibitions of animals that are not caught within this definition include where the animals are kept in a pet shop or at a circus, or on premises where members of the public have access on seven or more days in any consecutive 12 month period.

Other operations that require licensing include sea-life centres, butterfly collections, aviaries, centres for bird of prey and reptile collections. Pet and farm animal collections do not need a licence under the ZLA81.

Licences are granted for an initial period of four years and renewed at six-year intervals. The aim is to secure the dual objectives of enforcing minimum animal welfare standards and safeguarding the public who visit zoos.

An application for a zoo licence must be preceded by a notice of intention to the Local Authority; publication of the notice in both a local and national newspaper; and its public exhibition at the premises in question (S2). No application forms or notices have been prescribed but DEFRA have published recommended versions of these documents.

In considering the application, the Local Authority must take account of any representations made by various bodies comprising the police and fire authorities, national zoological institutions, the local planning authority as well as from the applicant himself. Other individuals can object if they feel the zoo would put at risk the health and safety of those living in the neighbourhood (S3).

A Council can only refuse to issue a licence for the reasons specified in the Act. These grounds are however comparatively extensive and includes the preservation of law and order and if the health and safety of residents would be injuriously affected (S4).

A licence may be refused if the standards of accommodation and staffing are inadequate for the proper care and well being of the animals. The criminal background of applicants and keepers can lead to rejection if they have been convicted of relevant offences.

Unlike most licensing regimes planning permission must be obtained before an application under the ZLA81. The Council must consider inspectors' reports before granting or refusing a licence. If granted, the licence must be publicly displayed at the zoo's public entrance. Conditions can be attached to zoo licences including those related to the following areas of concern:

- Precautions to be taken against the escape of animals, and steps to be taken in the event of any escape or unauthorised release.
- Records to be kept of the numbers of different animals, of acquisitions, births, deaths, disposals or escapes of animals, of the causes of any such deaths and the health of animals.
- Insurance against liability for damage caused by animals.

In addition to such conditions as the local authority think necessary or desirable, standard conditions, as recommended by the Secretary of State, should also be attached.

The management of zoos is outlined in the Secretary of State's Standards of Modern Zoo Practice (S9). These provide benchmark standards which cover the various aspects of animal care as well as post-mortem facilities, safety and security, and visitor facilities.

S7 provides a mechanism for the transfer, transmission and surrender of a licence. This allows the local authority to approve the transfer of a licence and to cancel a licence that is surrendered at any time by its holder. For a minimum period of three months after the death of a licence-holder, his personal representatives are deemed to be the licence holders, thus allowing the business to continue.

Animal Welfare Act 2006

The Animal Welfare Act 2006 has been described by DEFRA as *"the most comprehensive modernisation of laws on domestic and captive animals for a century"*. It will consolidate fragmented animal protection and modernise over 20 animal welfare laws relating to farmed and non-farmed animals. In summary, the Act will:

- Extend to companion animals welfare codes agreed by Parliament, a mechanism currently used to provide guidance on welfare for farmed animals.
- Strengthen penalties and amend current offences related to animal fighting.
- Increase the effectiveness of law enforcement for animal welfare offences.
- Increase from 12 to 16 the minimum age at which a child may buy an animal, and prohibit the giving of pets as prizes to unaccompanied children under the age of 16 (known as the "goldfish clause").
- Ban mutilations of animals, with certain specified exemptions.
- Reduce animal suffering by enabling preventive action to be taken.
- Place a duty on those responsible for domestic and companion animals to do all that is reasonable to ensure the welfare of their animals.
- Improve powers of inspection/entry.

7

Street Trading

Licensing Authorities have the power to control street trading (such as market stalls, craft fairs, burger vans and ice-cream vans) within their area. Licensing Authorities outside of London can resolve to designate streets under schedule 4 to the Local Government (Miscellaneous Provisions) Act 1982 as:

- A licence street - for formalised street markets, with established stalls on a regular basis.
- A consent street - for occasional street trading.
- A prohibited street - where no trading may take place.
- An undesignated street - street trading may take place without any controls in place.

What is Street Trading?

Street trading is the offering, exposing or selling of goods for sale (including living things). This means that the remit covers the advertising and offering of items for sale although – unlike the position in London – it is restricted only to goods and not to services.

Street trading in London is controlled by the London Local Authorities Act 1990 (as amended) and also the London Local Authorities Act 1996, which regulates occasional sales. Further private Acts have been passed to control street trading, such as in Leicester, Liverpool and Maidstone, which also provides powers to seize illegally sold goods (see 36 Licensing News 19 (November 2006)).

Street trading for these purposes involves the actual sale of goods, and not just an agreement to sell goods – that is, the goods need to be physically present and title in the property must pass as part of the contract transacted between the trader and the buyer. In Luke v Charles (1861) 25 JP 148 it was held that goods must be exposed for sale, not just for viewing.

The following are exempt from the street trading controls:

- Trading by a person acting as a pedlar with a pedlar's certificate granted under the Pedlars Act 1871 (see pedlars, below).
- Markets or fairs, where there is statutory authority to hold the market or fair (such as by way of royal charter).
- Trading in a trunk road picnic area provided by the Secretary of State under S112 of the Highways Act 1980 (HA80).
- Trading as a newsvendor (only newspapers or periodicals may be sold and no stall may be larger than 1m by 0.25m by 2m high and does not stand on the carriageway).
- Trading carried on at petrol garages or on their forecourts.
- Trading at premises used as a shop, or in a street adjoining those premises and which is part of the shop's business. This means that a shoe shop can display shoes outside, but could not, for example, sell ice-creams. In any event, there may be obstruction offences that may be committed under highways legislation.
- Selling things, or offering or exposing them for sale, as a roundsman. Following Kempin (t/a British Bulldog Ice Cream) v Brighton & Hove Council (The Times, 13 March 2001), ice-cream sales vans require street trading consents as they do not follow a specific round of customers to take orders and deliver order placed earlier. However, there is nothing to prevent a genuine roundsman from making ad-hoc sales on his route.
- The use for trading facilities or recreation or refreshment under the HA80, such as pavement cafes.
- Activities authorised by S5 of the Police, Factories, etc. (Miscellaneous Provisions) Act 1916, for charitable and benevolent purposes.

Street trading is also prohibited on special roads, such as motorways, motorway service areas, and principal trunk roads and a "street" is defined in the HA80 as including any road, footway, beach or other area to which the public have access without payment.

Pedlars

The Pedlars Act 1871 (as amended) (PA71) defines a pedlar as:

> *"Any hawker, pedlar, petty chapman, tinker, caster of metals, mender of chairs, or other person who, without any horse or other beast bearing or drawing burden, travels and trades on foot and goes from town to town or to other men's houses, carrying to sell or exposing for sale any goods, wares, or merchandise, or procuring orders for goods, wares, or merchandise immediately to be delivered, or selling or offering for sale his skill in handicraft".*

It is an offence to act as a pedlar without a Pedlar's Certificate. The certificates are granted by the police and the applicant must be:

- Over 17.
- Is a person of good character; and
- In good faith intends to carry on the trade of a pedlar.

Pedlar's Certificates remain in force for one year from the date of issue and certificates are not required by the following:

- Commercial travellers or other people selling or seeking orders for goods, wares, merchandise to or from people who are dealers therein and who buy to sell again, or selling or seeking orders for books as agents authorised in writing by the publishers of such books.
- Sellers of vegetables, fish, fruit, or victuals.
- People selling or exposing to sale goods, wares, or merchandise in any legally established market or fair.

Many police forces require applicants to supply photographs to be attached to the Pedlar's Certificates, but this is not a mandatory requirement. Equally, some police forces may maintain a central register of issued certificates, or more commonly these will be held at the police station or office where the certificate was issued. The current fee is £12.25.

Pedlars must be a person of good character (S5) however there is no further definition. Kent police suggest that this should be given a liberal interpretation provided that any decision where a person is deemed not to be of good character can be evidenced in writing. Any decision concerning the issue or otherwise of a certificate must comply with the Human Rights Act 1998 and a full record kept of the decision.

Any pedlar shall at all times, on demand, produce and show their certificate to the following:

- A Justice of the Peace.
- A police officer.
- Any person to whom such pedlar offers his goods for sale; or
- Any person in whose private grounds or premises such pedlar is found.

Any pedlar who refuses, on demand, to show their certificate to, and allow it to be read and copied commits an offence. The Police and Criminal Evidence Act 1984 (as amended by the Serious Organised Crime and Police Act 2005) applies to any police powers contained within the PA71.

Pedlars are able to enter on to private property unsolicitedly and speculatively. As the "Licensing Authority" the police have the responsibility of ensuring that the public are protected from unscrupulous people who use this to commit criminal activities. Only those who appear to genuinely intend pursuing legitimate business in a lawful manner should hold a Pedlar's Certificate.

Even if an offence has not been committed or proceeded with, a Magistrates' court may summon a pedlar and revoke their certificate if satisfied that they are not, in good faith, carrying on the business of a pedlar. This may be useful for licensing enforcement officers to deal with pedlars who have been in fact acting as street traders.

There have been a number of reported cases which have tried to provide a yardstick of when a pedlar stops acting as a pedlar and becomes a street trader. In Chichester District Council v Wood [1997] EWHC Admin 270, the Court held that:

- Each case depends on its own facts.
- A pedlar goes to his customers rather than allowing them to come to him.
- A pedlar trades as he travels rather than travels to trade.
- A pedlar is a pedestrian.
- A pedlar sells reasonably small items.
- He may use some small means of assisting in the transport of his goods, such as a trolley.
- The whole "apparatus of trading" needs to be considered if it is of such a scale to take the person out of the definition of pedlar.
- The use of a stall, stand or barrow may indicate an intention to be a street trader and to remain in one place or a succession of places.
- Setting up a stall or barrow and waiting for people to approach is an indication of a street trader rather than a pedlar. Case law seems to indicate that moving within a relatively small distance of 100 yards, or not moving far within a period of 10 minutes to 45 minutes, would generally indicate street trading and not peddling.

Designating Streets

A decision to pass a resolution to designate a street will usually be taken by the Council committee responsible for street trading, typically the licensing committee.

On deciding in principle to designate a street, the Council must advertise two consecutive weeks notice of its intention in a newspaper circulating in the district. It may be advisable to include a map of the proposal and place public notices in the affected streets.

The committee is under a duty to consider any representations and if they designate the street and a further public notice must be published at least 28 days before the resolution takes effect.

A designation may be reviewed and amended at any time, providing the statutory procedure is complied with. Licensing Authorities should be aware of the rights of existing traders if a change in a street's designation is likely to affect them.

Many Councils find it useful to state in their resolution that the designation includes the highway and "*x* metres from the footway" or "all adjoining alleyways, footways and thoroughfares", to include traders on the periphery of those streets.

It is also possible for a Licensing Authority to apply a particular policy towards street trading, either generally or in relation to specific streets, providing that it is prepared to allow for exceptions where appropriate (see Chapter 2 on Policy).

Street Trading

In addition to other details that may be required by the Council, applicants for street trading licences must state:

- Their full name and address.
- The street in which they wish to trade.
- The days and times in which they wish to trade.
- The articles they wish to sell and
- A description of the stall or container they wish to use.

The Council can also require two photographs of the applicant to be supplied.

Street trading licences may not be granted to anyone under 17, or when a control order under S7 of the Local Government (Miscellaneous Provisions) Act 1982 is in force, which prevents anyone from offering or exposing anything for sale on the highway or placing a stall or structure within 15m of the highway.

There is a duty on a Licensing Authority to grant and to renew a licence subject to the following:

- There is not enough space in the street for the applicant without causing undue interference or inconvenience to other users of the street.
- That there are already traders trading in the street from shops or

otherwise selling the goods the applicant wishes to.

- That the applicant wishes to trade for fewer days than the minimum the Licensing Authority has specified by resolution under paragraph 2(11)
- That the applicant is unsuitable by reason of having convicted of an offence of for any other reason.
- That the applicant has "persistently refused or neglected" to pay previous fees or charges due to the Council for either previous licences or services provided by the Council in his capacity as licence-holder.
- That the applicant has without reasonable excuse failed to avail themselves to a reasonable extent of a previous licence.

If the Licensing Authority has grounds for refusing the application because of lack of space in the street; existing competition; or because of a lack of use of a previous licence, it may consider limiting the licence to trade on fewer days or for a shorter period in each day, or may limit trading to only one or more of the types of article being proposed for sale. It is important to note in this respect that the Licensing Authority may only limit hours/times or types of goods sought – but not both – and traders cannot be limited to only selling one type of good.

Street trading licences must specify the place (including a specific spot in a street if deemed necessary), days and times during which trading may take place, and the articles that may be sold. These are the principal terms of the licence. Reasonable subsidiary terms may also be applied, which may stipulate the size and type of any stall or container to be used; require the stall-holders name or number to be displayed on the stall or container; and prohibiting or restricting where trade waste may be left.

The holder of a street trading licence may employ any other person to assist him without requiring further permission, although persons under 17 may not be employed if byelaws have been passed under S20 of the Children and Young Persons Act 1933 (as amended).

Street trading licences may not be granted for more than 12 months.

If a Council decides to re-designate a licence street as a consent street, then all street trading licences for that street cease to be of effect when the resolution takes effect. Local Authorities taking that route should be wary of the potential implications arising under the Human Rights Act 1988, as licences are effectively possessions under Article 1 to the First Protocol to the European Convention on Human Rights, and cannot be taken away except in the public interest.

A street trading licence can be revoked at any time if the Council is of the opinion that since granting or renewing the licence there is no longer any space in the street for the trader without causing undue interference or inconvenience to other users of the street; or the licence-holder has been convicted of an offence or for any other reason; or because the licence-holder has persistently refused or neglected to pay fees due to the Council for it or charges due to them as reasonable charges for collecting refuse; cleaning streets and other services rendered to him as a licence-holder; or if the licence-holder has not used the licence to a reasonable extent without reasonable excuse.

In addition to revoking a licence on the above grounds, a Licensing Authority can vary its principal terms, refuse to grant or renew the licence; grant a licence on different principal terms to those sought in the application; or limit the trader to a particular place in a street.

A specific procedure is set out before any of these courses of action may be undertaken:

- A notice must be served on the licence-holder/applicant.
- The grounds on which the decision would be based must be specified.
- The applicant must have the opportunity of making written representations within seven days of receiving the notice.
- The matter may not determine until either representations are made; the period for making representations has lapsed; or representations were not made within the required period.

Street Trading Consents

Street trading consents are a more flexible system of control, designed for more ad-hoc trading than the formalised system typified by street trading licences.

Applications for the grant or renewal of consents must be made in writing, and may not be granted to a person under 17, or for trading in a highway where a control order is made under the 1976 Act (the same pre-conditions that apply to street trading licences).

There is no standard form and Licensing Authorities frequently ask for appropriate levels of public liability insurance, photographs of the applicant, a site plan or map of the proposed trading location, and a statutory declaration of any previous criminal convictions.

Unlike street trading licences, there is no duty to hear oral representations from applications for street trading consents, nor is there any duty to give reasons. Best practice would suggest that however applicants are given the opportunity to make representations, and that reasons for the refusal of an application are given when appropriate: see R v Bristol City Council, ex parte Pearce and another (The Times, 7 December 1984). In that case, which pre-dated the Human Rights Act 1998, a street trader was held not to have a legal right to his street trading consent, and did not have an expectation that it would be granted. This may be decided differently nowadays, although the court also ruled that Licensing Authorities should follow the rules of natural justice by allowing applicants the opportunity to comment on the nature of representations made against their applicant.

It has been argued by some that a refusal to grant a street trading licence is amenable to judicial review, and this provides the appeal mechanism. However, the European Court of Justice ruled in Tsfayo v United Kingdom (The Times, 23 November 2006) that judicial review was not an independent appeal route from a Local Authority housing benefit and Council benefit review board, and so a similar argument could be invoked in relation to street trading consents.

Licensing Authorities have a wide discretion to attach conditions, which can be varied at any time and which also include those to:

- Prevent obstruction of the street or danger to people using it.
- Nuisance or annoyance (whether to persons using the street or local residents and other occupants).

Specific permission must be given in the consent if the trader is to be allowed to trade from a van or other vehicle, or from a stall, barrow, cart or portable stall (see paragraphs 7(7) and (8) of the schedule). Where consent is granted, it can be conditional that the licence-holder trades from a specific site, and the times or other periods during which they may trade. No street trading consent can be granted for longer than 12 months at a time, and the holder may surrender it any time at which point its' validity ceases – the Licensing Authority must refund the unused portion of any surrendered or revoked street trading consent.

The holder of a street trading consent may also employ others with the same caveat which relates to licences.

Conditions

Conditions may be attached to street trading licences and consents, such as:

- Trading hours.
- The goods to be sold.
- The location of the stalls.
- Noise control.
- Storage and disposal of litter.
- Type of stall, barrow, or vehicle that may be used.

In addition, certain conditions must be added to street trading licences (but not consents):

- The street in which, days on which and times between which trading may take place.
- A description of the articles that are permitted to be sold and
- The specific place that trading may take place from, where this is designated by the Licensing Authority.

Other conditions can relate to the size and type of any stall or container to be used for street trading; require that the stall and container shall carry the licence-holder's name and/or number, and prohibit the licence-holder from leaving refuse, restricting where it can be left, or how much may be left.

Fees

Licensing Authorities may set fees which cover their reasonable costs of enforcing and administering the system of street trading consents: see R v Manchester City Council, ex parte King (*The Times,* 3 April 1991), where the High Court ruled that licensing income must not be used to raise revenue for the Council generally. In the case of street trading licences, fees can include the costs of refuse collection, street cleansing and other services provided to him as a street trader. These fees can either be recovered as one fee, or separately.

Different fees may be set for different types of licences or consent, and this can depend on:

- The duration of the licence or consent.
- The street to which it applies.
- The nature of the goods being authorised for sale.

The additional charges to licence-holders must be published in a local newspaper before they are changed, giving a reasonable period for representations to be made and considered in relation to them.

When accepting applications, a Licensing Authority can require part or the entire fee to be paid as a deposit, which will be refunded, should the application be refused.

If a licence is surrendered or revoked, the licence-holder may have his fee and any other charges remitted in whole or part.

8

Hearings & Appeals

By the very nature of the activities which require licensing it is inevitable that disagreements will sometimes arise. In cases concerning statutory authorities disagreements and concerns can often be addressed through discussion and some licensing regimes allow officers, under delegated powers, to grant the subsequent licence. When agreement can not be reached then many licensing regimes introduce a third party involvement, usually in the form of a hearing.

A fundamental principle of any licensing system is the right to a fair hearing with the safeguard of appeal. Such hearings are normally conducted by laypeople or experts depending on the licence and may take the form of written representations or more usually for licensing an oral hearing.

The right to a fair hearing is enshrined in the Human Rights Act (HRA) and for a hearing to be considered fair then the parties must have:

- Prior notice with precise details of the complaint and the procedure.
- The opportunity to attend, be allowed to present their case and be able to call witnesses.
- The fair conduct of the hearing without bias.
- The right to representation.
- Notification of the decision and the reasons for it.

The length of prior notice may be prescribed in the respective law together with the content of the notice. The period and information is designed to allow all parties sufficient time to prepare their respective cases.

Parties would normally have a right to attend, or in the case of written representations supply written evidence, to the person or body considering the application. In the case of an oral hearing it is usual for parties to be allowed to present their case and call witnesses to help support their evidence.

The hearing should be fair and without bias. Parties should be given equal opportunity and the matter considered by a third party who is not biased. The Courts have defined bias as *"where a fair minded and informed observer, having considered the facts, would conclude that there was a real possibility that the decision maker/body was biased"*. Porter v Magill (2001) UKHL 67.

To ensure no one is disadvantaged due to their presentation skills, or lack of understanding of the process, parties have the right to representation. In a Court such representation must be by a practising Solicitor or Barrister however at Council hearings this is not necessary and parties are free to nominate anyone to help them present their case.

All parties to a hearing must be advised of the decision and the reasons for the decision.

This was clearly established in the case of R v Burton-upon-Trent Justices ex parte Hussain 1996 DC where the Magistrates had specified the statutory grounds for non-renewal of a licence, but had not given reasons as to why those grounds had been met. The High Court made it clear that they should have done so, and also stated that had the matter been an appeal from the Local Authority, exactly the same requirements would apply.

Whilst that is the position for all licensing decisions, the Government has restated it in the Guidance for the LA03 states that *"it is important that licensing authorities should give comprehensive reasons for its decisions. Failure to give adequate reasons could itself give rise to grounds for an appeal. It is particularly important that reasons should also address the extent to which the decision has been made with regard to the Licensing Authority's statement of policy and this Guidance"* (para 10.9).

Hearings may be necessary for the:

- Initial grant of a licence.

- Review of an existing licence (LA03 & GA05).
- Actions against a licence – suspension or evocation, application of new conditions.
- Renewal of a licence.

The function of the hearing is to:

- Correctly identify, interpret and apply the law.
- Correctly identify and examine the facts and evidence.
- Follow correct procedures.
- Based on the above decide on the matter.

The Licensing Committee, as laypersons, should normally have access to a legal advice from the Council Legal Department. For Magistrates the Consolidated Criminal Practice Direction (Lord Chief Justice, March 2006) states *"At any time justices are entitled to receive advice to assist them in discharging their responsibilities. If they are in any doubt as to the evidence which has been given, they should seek the aid of their legal adviser"*. The Direction also advises that legal representatives only comment on:

- Questions of law.
- Questions of mixed law and fact.
- Matters of practice and procedure.
- Range of penalties available *(options available to the Committee)*.
- Relevant decisions of higher Courts.
- Guidance and/or policy.
- Other relevant issues.
- Decision making structure.

In Court any legal advice given in the closed session of a hearing should be repeated in the open session to give all parties the opportunity to comment on the advice given, and this is good practice in a Council committee.

LA03 and GA05 applications will be considered by the committee established under S6 of the LA03. This committee must consist of between 10 and 15 Councillors from which any number of three member sub committees are formed. Other matters can be considered by other committees established under the Local Government Act 1972. Licensing matters are Council, not Cabinet or Executive functions. The Local Government and Housing Act 1989 requires political balance on committees and sub committees although this does not apply to the LA03 Licensing committee.

LA03 and GA05 Hearings

The conduct of hearings for the LA03 is prescribed in the LA03 (Hearings) Regulations 2005 (referred to from now as the Hearings Regulations). The Hearings Regulations include the following general provisions about hearings:

- Timescales (R4).
- Notice of hearing and information (R6/7).
- Hearing in public (R14).
- Rights of attendance (R15/16).
- Procedure (R21).
- Determination and notification (R20/26/28).

Similar (but not identical) regulations under the GA05 (The Gambling (Hearings) Regulations) prescribe a number of factors for premises application hearings under this legislation.

The LA03 (S9) allows the Licensing committee to delegate decisions to a sub committee of three. Neither the Act nor Hearings Regulations specify the minimum number for the sub committee to be quorate it is therefore a matter for the Licensing Authority to determine with Kolvin et al commenting that *"a common misconception is that the sub committee must consist of three members actually sitting"*. (Kolvin* p44). LACORS (Licensing Committee Hearings under the LA03, March 2005) suggests that in the interests of a fair hearing, and principles of accountability and public decision-making, that the sub committee does not proceed with less than three members. In practice necessity may occasionally require two member committees, provided the Council constitution allows this.

Although the Hearings Regulations prescribed a number of actions for LA03 applications they do not lay down a procedure for licensing hearings. R21 states that the *"Authority shall determine the procedure to be followed"* and R23 that the *"hearing shall take the form of a discussion led by the authority and cross examination shall not be permitted"*, unless the authority consider it necessary to establish the facts from either party.

LACORS (Licensing Committee Hearings under the LA03, March 2005) recommend the following model procedure:

- Chair opens the meeting, introducing Members of the committee and officers present to the applicant and members of the public, explains the nature of the decision to be taken, and the procedure to be followed.
- The officer outlines the application, any relevant representations and relevancies to the Local Authority licensing policy statement and statutory guidance (optional).
- Members to ask any relevant questions of the officer.
- Licensing officer introduces applicant (if present) and invites him or her, or person representing them, to address the committee or clarify any information arising from the officers' outline, if necessary.
- Licensing officer to invite those parties making representations to address the sub committee.
- Members to ask any relevant questions of those parties making representations.
- Applicant or person representing them to ask any relevant questions of those parties making representations.
- If necessary, the committee will consider requests to allow other parties invited by the applicant to address the committee.
- Applicant or person representing them addresses the committee.
- Members may ask any relevant questions of the applicant or person representing them.
- Parties that made representations to ask any relevant questions of the applicant or person representing them.
- Chair to invite applicant or those representing them, and any parties making representations, to briefly summarise their points if they wish.
- Chair asks all parties that they are satisfied they have said all they wish to.
- Members of the committee discuss and make their decision.

- Chair relays the decision and the reasons given for the decision, and any conditions placed upon the licence (if granted) and the licensing objective that they relate to.

It is good practice for any oral hearing for the chairman to outline the procedure to be followed to ensure all parties are aware of the process. For LA03 applications this is also a legal requirement under R22 which states *"At the beginning of the hearing, the authority shall explain to the parties the procedure which it proposes to follow"*.

For LA03 applications the committee shall disregard any information which is not relevant to:

- The application, and
- The promotion of the licensing objectives.

Manchester et al consider that R19 is drafted to prevent parties from *"introducing new grounds or raising completely different mattes at the hearing to those contained in their representations, rather than requiring the authority to disregard anything that is not specially addressed in the representation"* (Manchester p51).

The LA03 Guidance states that *"as a matter of practice, Licensing Authorities should seek to focus the hearing on the steps needed to promote the particular licensing objectives which has given rise to the specific representation and avoid straying into undisputed areas"* (para 5.68). The LA03 Guidance also states *"it is not the role of a Licensing Authority to determine the guilt or innocence of individuals charged with licensing or other offences committed on licensed premises. There is therefore no reason why representations giving rise to a review of a premises licence need be delayed pending the outcome of any criminal proceedings"* (para 5.114).

For the LA03 the Hearings Regulations prescribe a number of specific requirements. The maximum time period for holding the hearing is typically 20 working days other than a Review, following closure order under S167 (ten days) and a counter notice following police objection to TEN (seven days).

Under R6 the notice period for a hearing is two working days, other than a review hearing following a S167 closure, in which case the period is five working days. Notices must be served to the persons listed in Schedule 2 of the Hearings Regulations namely the applicant, the police and anyone making relevant representations.

Information to accompany the notice is prescribed in R7 as follows:

- The procedure for hearing.
- Copy of relevant representations.
- Copy of any relevant police notices.
- Rights of those attending (R15/16).
- That the Council may determine the application in their absence (R20).

In determining an application the Licensing committee must consider:

- The statement of policy.
- S182 Guidance.
- The argument and evidence presented by all parties.
- Steps that are necessary to promote the licensing objectives.

For LA03 applications the committee may take any of the following steps including on review in brackets:

- Grant.
- Reject.
- Grant with conditions.
- Modify the conditions of the licence i.e. reducing hours (review).
- Exclude a licensable activity i.e. playing of live music (review).
- Remove the DPS, if they consider that the problems are the result of poor management (review).
- Suspend the licence for a period not exceeding three months (review).
- To revoke the licence (review).

The Institute of Licensing (IoL) have introduced a general Code of Practice for imposing licence conditions which includes:

- Conditions must satisfy the tests of necessity and reasonableness and must directly relate to the harm being addressed.
- A condition must be proportionate to the identified risk, and should not require disproportionate resources in order to comply with it. It should be consistent with the practice, as far as reasonably practicable, of other licensing authorities and recognised good practice.
- Conditions should not duplicate other enforcement regimes. Before a condition is imposed consideration should be given as to whether alternative means are available to address the risk, including obligations imposed by other statutory requirements.
- Conditions shall, as far as possible, be written in plain English.

The LA03 (S183) specifically prevents the Council for making orders relating to costs.

The Council must determine the application within five working days of the hearing (R26), other than for a TEN when the decision must be announced at the end of the meeting. All parties must be notified of the decision without delay and they must be told of their rights of appeal (R29).

Non LA03 and GA05 Hearings

All other areas of licensing and registration administered by Local Authorities allow the Council to decide on its own procedures, as there are no statutory provisions beyond those relating to all committee meetings required by the Local Government Act 1972. Provided any such hearings comply with the following basic requirements, the actual procedure is left to the Council to decide. The overriding necessities are:

- Compliance with the rules of natural justice.
- Consideration of Human Rights issues; and
- Decisions in accordance with "Wednesbury" principles.

The procedure itself should be adopted, and thereafter kept under regular review to ensure that it remains relevant and workable. That procedure should be communicated to all parties and available to any interested member of the public.

Role of the Chair

The Chair of the licensing committee has a crucial role to ensure everyone understands the process and the committee is conducted in fair manner. At St Albans City and District Council the legal advisor, Judith Adamson, adopts a light-hearted approach to the topic. She issues the Licensing committee Chairman with the "10 Commandments" (adapted with permission of Bedfordshire Magistrates Courts).

- Thou shalt control thy hearing with confidence.
- Thou shalt ask thy licensing lawyer if thy needeth legal advice.
- Thou shalt provide a length of time for each party to speaketh.
- Thou shalt think along structured lines.
- Thou shalt lead thy team, but only in the knowledge that thy vote carries no greater weight than thy wingers.
- Thou shalt be silent most of the time.
- Thou shalt commit no discourtesy.
- Thou shalt at all times be aware of the perception that others will have of what you are saying.
- Thou shalt be very sparing with thine humour.
- Thou shalt never think thou knowest it all.

Appeals

All legal processes must allow the challenge of decisions to an independent and higher judicial authority. For appeals against Council licensing decisions there are five main options:

- Magistrates Court.
- Crown Court: either at first instance or on appeal.
- Case stated to the High Court.
- Judicial Review.
- Local Government Ombudsman (not judicial and decisions are not binding on the Council concerned).

Until 2008 the ultimate Court in the UK is the House of Lords however this will change with the implementation of the Constitutional Reform Act 2005. This Act completes the separation of the legal system from Government and Parliament by reforming the role of the Lord Chancellor, establishing a Supreme Court and an independent Judicial Appointments Commission.

The vast majority of appeals for premises-based licensing and taxi licensing will be considered by the local Magistrates. Appeals must be made within the time laid down in the relevant legislation governing the area of licensing concerned, and there is no set form or procedure. However some Courts have created a standard form. A fee is payable on lodging an appeal.

The Court will normally arrange an initial appeal hearing within 28 days to decide whether there is a case to hear and arrange a full hearing when sufficient court time can be allowed. At the full hearing in relation to appeals under LA03 the Magistrates may:

- Dismiss the appeal.
- Substitute the decision.
- Send the case back to the Council with directions.

In other areas the options open to the Magistrates on appeal will depend on the way the complaint is worded, which means that care must be take when drafting the complaint itself.

The Court may also make such costs orders as it considers fit however the Magistrates Association and the Justices' Clerks Society has advised that awarding costs for a licensing appeal should be an exception and not a rule. This follows the case of Bradford v Booth [2000] C.O.D. 338 DC.

For the LA03 S181 and Schedule 5 allow appeals against PLs (part 1), CPC (part 2), TEN (part 3), PersL (part 3) and Closure orders (part 3) may appeal within 21 days of notification.

The LA03 Guidance states *"In hearing an appeal against any decision made by a Licensing Authority, the Magistrates' Court concerned will have regard to that Licensing Authority's statement of licensing policy and this Guidance. However, the court would be entitled to depart from either the statement of licensing policy or this Guidance if it considered it is justified to do so because of the individual circumstances of any case. In other words, while the appellate court will normally consider the matter as if it was "standing in the shoes" of the Licensing Authority, it would be entitled to find that the Licensing Authority should have departed from its own policy or the Guidance because the particular circumstances would have justified such a decision by the Licensing Authority"* (para 10.8).

Schedule 5 specifically states that for appeals brought by interested parties then in addition to the Licensing Authority the applicant is also a respondent. This allows the applicant to address the Court and call their own witnesses. The LA03 does not state the same automatic right for interested parties if an applicant appeals. There is no binding case law however two Magistrates Courts have consider the matter and reached different conclusions. At Horseferry Road Magistrates (Lucas v Westminster City Council, 2005) the Court allowed the residents to be joined as respondents however at Redhill Magistrates Court (Woldingham Golf Course v Tandridge District Council, 2005) the Court would not accept the arguments used for Lucas.

The implementation of a decision depends on whether this will restrict a current right ie reduce current operating hours. If the answer is yes then the law will allow a right of appeal to heard before the restriction may be enforced ie S52 of the LA03. S52 Road Safety Act has altered this for taxi licensing to allow driver suspensions or revocations to have immediate effect if necessary in the interests of public safety.

A number of licensing regimes include specialist appeal processes.

Taxi licensing - All appeals are heard by the Magistrates Court, and an appeal must be brought within 21 days of the date of the decision. There is one exception to this which is an appeal against a refusal to grant a

Hackney Carriage Proprietors' Licence which is commenced in the Crown Court (S7 Public Health Acts (Amendment) Act 1907). The appeal period for the Crown Court is 28 days from the date of the decision by the Council. There is a further right of appeal to the Crown Court (within 21 days of the Magistrates decision) against all the decisions of the Magistrates.

Gambling Act - The GA05 establishes the Gambling Appeals Tribunal to consider appeals against Gambling Commission decisions for operating and personal licences. Applications must be made within one month of decision with further appeal to the High Court. Premises Licences appeals will be heard by the Magistrates, and application must be made within 21 days of the date of the Licensing Authority's decision (S207 GA05).

Civil Marriage Premises - The Marriages (Approved Premises) Regulations 1995 allow for an internal review by the Licensing Authority of its own decision. In such a case R9 states that "neither an officer nor any member of a committee or sub committee of the authority which made the decision on behalf of the authority shall take part in the decision on the review". The internal review may:

- Confirm the original decision.
- Vary conditions.
- Substitute the decision.

HMO's - For a refusal of an HMO licence an appeal must be made within 28 days to the Residential Property Tribunal Service (RPTS). The RPTS provides an independent tribunal service in England for settling disputes involving private rented property.

Planning and Building Regulations - Due to the technical nature of both planning and building control, disputes are considered by independent specialists appointed by the Secretary of State with appeals restricted to the applicant. Planning decisions may be appealed to the Planning Inspectorate within six months. The appeal may take the form of written representations or for complex cases a local inquiry. For building regulation disputes the Building Act 1984 allows for "determinations" and "appeals" to the SoS. Such disputes may arise with either the Council or a private approved inspector. Determinations relate to questions of compliance of full plans applications with the requirements of the Building Regulations and appeals relate to decisions by a Local Authority to refuse applications to relax requirements.

Judicial Review

In certain circumstance parties will have access to the High Court by way of Judicial Review (JR) to challenge the lawfulness of a decision or action made by a public body. The sort of public bodies whose decisions may be challenged include:

- Government departments.
- Local authorities.
- Health authorities.
- Chief constables and police authorities.
- Magistrates, coroners and county courts.

JR is normally only available if there is no alternative action which could solve the problem. The process involves two stages as the court must first give permission if it is considers there is a case to be heard and the application is within time periods. Claims for JR must be brought promptly (within three months of the event/decision) and will only consider whether the decision was "lawful" i.e. excess of power, abdication of power, abuse of power, improper purpose, procedural impropriety or incompatibly with the Human Rights Act.

Before making a claim, the claimant should send a letter to the defendant. The purpose of this letter is to identify the issues in dispute and establish whether litigation can be avoided. The Ministry of Justice web site (www.justice.gov.uk) provides an outline of a pre-action letter which should include the following information:

- Details of the claimant.
- Reference details.
- The details of the matter being challenged.
- The date of the decision with a brief summary of the facts and why it is contended to be wrong.
- The details of the action that the defendant is expected to take.
- The details of any legal advisers.
- The details of any interested parties.
- The details of any information sought.
- The details of any documents that are considered relevant and necessary.

- The address for reply and service of court documents.
- Proposed reply date (normally 14 days).

In responding to this proposed claim the defendant should set out whether the issue in question is conceded in part, or in full, or will be contested.

Based on this information the Court will decide if there is a case to be heard and if an application for JR is successful, the court can make of one of six orders:

- Quashing order.
- Prohibiting order.
- Mandatory order.
- Declaration.
- Injunction and/or
- Damages.

The most common in licensing is a quashing order which overturns an invalid decision. The public body must then take the decision again applying the proper legal test or following the correct procedure.

Case Stated

S61 of the Access to Justice Act 1999 allows for a case to be referred to the High Court, as a case stated.

The lower court must state the case for the decision reached, expressing the facts of the case and the legal issues considered. This form of appeal may only be used to challenge a decision made on points of law, not on points of fact.

A High Court can refuse to state a case if the application is frivolous or on procedural grounds such as a failure to observe time limits. JR is an option for unreasonable refusal.

9

Other Premises Licensing

This chapter covers the following premises based licensing regimes:

- HMO.
- Civil marriage premises.
- Sex establishments.
- Firearms certificates.
- Scrap metal dealers.

HMO Licensing

Following the report "Quality & Choice: A Decent Home for All" in 1999 the Housing Act 2004 (HA04) introduced compulsory licensing for Houses in Multiple Occupation (HMO). The Act also brought in "home information packs" and certain responsibilities of those selling houses.

The HMO licensing regime seeks to ensure that:

- Landlords or agents etc are fit and proper persons.
- The standards of tenancy/property management are adequate.
- Local Housing Authorities (LHA's) have measures available to ensure landlords cooperate.
- Where landlords are unwilling/unable to meet the standards LHAs can step in to manage properties.
- Vulnerable tenants can be protected.
- High risk HMOs are identified, so that enforcement can be targeted.

For England (Wales will introduce its own legislation) all HMOs must be managed in accordance with management regulations (The Management of HMO (England) Regulations 2006), whether they need a licence or not. HMOs comprising of three or more storeys and occupied by five or more persons from at least two households must be licensed. The standard test for an HMO is defined in the Licensing of HMO (Prescribed Descriptions) Order 2006 as:

- One or more units which are not self-contained flats.
- The living accommodation is occupied by more than a single household as their main residence (this includes students).
- Their occupation of the living accommodation is the only use of that accommodation.
- Rents are payable.
- Two or more of the households share basic amenities, such as a kitchen, or the living accommodation is lacking in basic amenities.

A storey includes basements and attics if they are occupied or have been converted for occupation. Commercial premises on the ground or any upper floor are also included in the calculation of the number of storeys.

The following buildings are exempt from needing a licence (HA04 Sch 14):

- Buildings managed by LHA's, Registered Social Landlords, police, fire or health authority or regulated by other Acts.
- Student accommodation managed by a college with an "Approved Code".
- Buildings occupied by religious communities.
- Owner-occupied (with no more than two others) or buildings occupied by only two persons.
- Children's homes, care homes and residential family centres.
- Boarding schools.
- Prisons and remand centres etc.

LHA's may also extend the licensing regime to cover smaller HMO's if they consider a significant proportion are not well managed. Any LHA extending the scheme or standards (S56) must carry out full consultation (see Chapter 2) with any persons likely to be effected and they must have regard to the:

- Housing strategy and homelessness.
- Whether the designation will significantly help the problems.
- Any other courses of action available to them.

Any extension must be confirmed by the Secretary of State or fall within a specific designation (S58). Once approved the designation will last for a maximum of five years the LHA must publish a notice stating (S59):

- That the designation has been made and the date it comes into force.
- How the scheme was approved.
- Any other prescribed information.

The law intends to improve standards by regulations to cover the following aspects:

- Living accommodation, windows and ventilation.
- Fire safety.
- Safe supply of gas, electricity and lighting.
- Water supply and drainage.
- Installations for cleaning, sanitation and food storage are kept in good repair.
- Disposal of rubbish.
- Display of notices and occupiers given procedures and contact details in case of emergency.
- Common parts are maintained and cleaned.
- Occupiers do not frustrate the manager in complying with obligations under the regulations.

There are national minimum standards laid down in the Licensing and Management of HMO and Other Houses (Miscellaneous Provisions) (England) Regulations 2006 which define "reasonably suitable" however these standards may be amended by the LHA to reflect local conditions. If the LHA amend the standards they must ensure they are proportionate and consistent with national standards. The standards cover:

- Heating.
- Washing.
- Kitchens.
- Fire precautionary facilities.

The application for a licence is to the LHA and must include the following information (Schedule 3):

- Name of landlord and/or agent.
- Property details, including the number of rooms in use.
- Date of conversion of the property (if relevant).
- Number of households and individuals.
- Details of fire precautions and safety certificates.
- Prescribed information on the applicant (last five years).

LHAs may also ask for additional information provided it is necessary to carry out their licensing functions and they may set their own fees. There is no statutory time limit on the processing of applications and when deciding the LHA must consider whether (S64):

- The property is reasonably suitable for the proposed use.
- The proposed licence holder is fit and proper person and the most appropriate person to hold the licence.
- Any proposed manager of the property is the person having control of the property, or an agent.
- Any proposed manager of the property is a fit and proper person.
- The proposed management arrangements are satisfactory.

In deciding whether a landlord or agent is "fit and proper" the relevant offences are:

- Fraud, dishonesty, violence, drugs or certain sexual offences.
- Unlawful discrimination.
- Housing or landlord and tenant law.

Before determining a licence application the LHA must serve a notice (with copy of approval or rejection) on the applicant, any person with an interest in the property or any person affected by any conditions. They have 14 days to respond.

The licence is for each property and last for a maximum of five years. The LHA must include the following conditions (Schedule 4):

- Produce gas safety certificate annually (where appropriate).
- Keep electrical appliances and furniture in safe condition and supply the LHA on demand with a declaration as to the safety of the same.
- Install and maintain smoke alarms in working order and supply the LHA on demand with a declaration as to the same.
- Provide occupiers with written statement of terms.

The LHA may also include conditions which:

- Restrict the use or occupation of parts of the property.
- Require reasonable steps to be taken to reduce anti-social behaviour.
- Require steps to be taken to comply with the HMO suitability standards and time limits for such compliance.
- Require the attendance of training on codes of practice.

The LHA may revoke a licence if there have been breaches of a licence condition or the licence holder or management is no longer a "fit and proper person". The procedure and notice periods are similar to the application stage.

On request the LHA may allow landlords a period of three or six months if they plan to end the use of the building as a licensed HMO. A Temporary Exemption Notice (TEN) under S62 exempts that property from being licensed for a period of three months and this may be extended to a max of six months in exceptional circumstances. This process may be used on the death of the licence holder when the property is to be treated as if a TEN had been served or on the sale of a property when the new owner may apply for a TEN.

LHAs must maintain a public register (S232) of all:

- Licences.
- TEN.
- Management Orders.

Civil Marriage Premises

S1 of The Marriage Act 1994 amended the Marriage Act 1949 to enable civil marriages to be solemnized on premises approved by the County Council, Metropolitan District Council or London Borough Councils.

The Marriages (Approved Premises) Regulations 1995 set the standards for premises stating that an application must include:

- The name and address of the applicant.
- Such information as the Council may reasonably require.
- A plan of the premises defining the rooms for marriages.
- A fee.

For premises to be considered suitable it must meet the requirements in Schedule 1 of the Regulations, namely:

- Having regard to their primary use, situation, construction and state of repair, the premises must, in the opinion of the authority, be a seemly and dignified venue for the solemnization of marriages.
- The premises must be regularly available to the public for use for the solemnization of marriages.
- The premises must have the benefit of such fire precautions as may reasonably be required by the authority, having consulted with the fire authority, and such other reasonable provision for the health and safety of persons employed in or visiting the premises as the authority considers appropriate.
- The premises must have no recent or continuing connection with any religion, religious practice or religious persuasion which would be incompatible with the use of the premises for the solemnization of marriages in pursuance of S26.
- The room or rooms in which ceremonies of marriage will be solemnized if approval is granted must be identifiable by description as a distinct part of the premises.

The Council will then inspect the premises and they must ensure that:

- The application and plans are available for public inspection and
- That a public notice has been placed in a newspaper.

The consultation period lasts for 21 days after which the Council may grant or refuse the application. The licence lasts for three years and the Council must attach the conditions stated in Schedule 2 of the Regulations, namely:

- The holder of the approval must ensure that there is at all times an individual with responsibility for ensuring compliance with these conditions ("the responsible person") and that the responsible persons occupation, seniority, position of responsibility in relation to the premises, or other factors (his "qualification"), indicate that he is in a position to ensure compliance with these conditions.
- The responsible person or, in his absence, an appropriately qualified deputy appointed by him, shall be available on the premises for a minimum of one hour prior to each marriage ceremony and throughout each marriage ceremony.
- The holder must notify the authority:
  (a) of his name and address immediately upon him becoming the holder of an approval under R7, and
  (b) of the name, address and qualification of the responsible person immediately upon the appointment of a new responsible person.
- The holder must notify the authority immediately of any change to any of the following—
  (a) the layout of the premises, as shown in the plan submitted with the approved application, or in the use of the premises,
  (b) the name or full postal address of the approved premises,
  (c) the description of the room or rooms in which marriages are to be solemnized,
  (d) the name or address of the holder of the approval, and
  (e) the name, address or qualification of the responsible person.
- The approved premises must be made available at all reasonable times for inspection by the authority.
- A suitable notice stating that the premises have been approved for the solemnization of marriages in pursuance of S26 of the

Marriage Act 1949 and identifying and giving directions to the room in which a marriage ceremony is to take place must be displayed at each public entrance to the premises for one hour prior to the ceremony and throughout the ceremony.

- No food or drink may be sold or consumed in the room in which a marriage ceremony takes place for one hour prior to that ceremony or during that ceremony.
- All marriage ceremonies must take place in a room which was identified as one to be used for the solemnization of marriages on the plan submitted with the approved application.
- The room in which a marriage is solemnized must be separate from any other activity on the premises at the time of the ceremony.
- The arrangements for and content of each marriage ceremony must meet with the prior approval of the superintendent registrar of the district in which the approved premises are situated.
- Any reading, music, words or performance which forms part of a ceremony of marriage celebrated on the premises must be secular in nature; for this purpose any such material used by way of introduction to, in any interval between parts of, or by way of conclusion to the ceremony shall be treated as forming part of the ceremony.
- Public access to any ceremony of marriage solemnized in approved premises must be permitted without charge.
- Any reference to the approval of premises on any sign or notice, or on any stationery or publication, or within any advertisement may state that the premises have been approved by the authority as a venue for marriage in pursuance of S26 of the Act, but shall not state or imply any recommendation of the premises or its facilities by the authority, the Registrar General or any of the officers or employees of either of them.

The Council may also attach conditions to ensure that use of the premises *"does not give rise to a nuisance of any kind"*.

The Council may also refuse an application if it considers the premises does not meet the requirements of Schedule 1 or having regard to the number of other approved premises in its area, that the superintendent registrar and a registrar are unlikely to be available regularly to attend the solemnization of marriages on the premises.

Regulation 12 allows the Council to set fees which reasonably represent the costs incurred.

Regulation 9 makes provision for an internal review if the applicant is not satisfied with the decision. The regulations state that *"The proper officer shall forthwith arrange for review of the decision by the authority and neither an officer nor any member of a committee or sub-committee of the authority which made the decision on behalf of the authority shall take part in the decision on the review"*

Councils may also revoke a licence if they are satisfied that the applicant has failed to meet the conditions or that the premises do not meet the requirements of Schedule 1. The Council must serve a notice giving a minimum 14 days and the applicant may make written representations. The decision is also subject to the internal review procedure.

Sex Establishments

S2 of The Local Government (Miscellaneous Provisions) Act 1982 (LGMPA82), allows District Councils to resolve to adopt Schedule 3 to the Act. Once in force, the Council can licence:

- Sex cinemas.
- Sex shops.

If the LGMPA82 Schedule 3 is not adopted, the Council has no control over these types of premises (In Greater London, the provisions of Greater London Council (General Powers) Act 1986 allow the London Borough Councils to adopt an amendment to Schedule 3 to the 1982 Act which allows them to licence sex encounter establishments).

The resolution must be passed at least a month before the adoption takes effect, and the Council must publish a notice that the resolution has been passed for two consecutive weeks in a local newspaper.

A sex shop or cinema is any premises, vehicle, vessel or stall used for a business that consists to a significant degree of display of R18 films (Sex Cinema) or selling, hiring, exchanging, lending, displaying or demonstrating sex articles (Sex Shop). Sex articles are items intended to:

- Simulate or encourage sexual activity or
- Acts of force or restraint associated with sexual activity.

Determining a "significant degree" of sex article sales is a continuing and contentious area of debate. Many matters may amount to material factors to be taken into account when making a decision, including the ratio of sex articles to other articles, the quantity of sales, and the nature of any displays. In London Borough of Lambeth v Grewel (1986) 84 LGR 538, the High Court held that the defendant's turnover of under 2% of stock was not a significant amount. In Watford Borough Council v Private Alternative Birth Control and Education Centres [1985] Crim LR 594 the High Court held that *"significant must mean something which signifies, something which is not insignificant, perhaps something which cannot be dismissed under the de minimis rule"*. Therefore, it will be a matter of fact in each case as to whether or not a licence is required, but small or trivial quantities can be safely disregarded.

Sex cinemas are defined in LGMPA82 Schedule 3 and do not include private residences where the public are not admitted or where a premises licence under the Licensing Act 2003 authorising exhibitions of films is in force.

Under the Video Recordings Act 1984, R18-rated films may only be sold from licensed sex shops, which can cause problems for non-specialist shops such as video hire shops or newsagents who would have to obtain a sex establishment licence even if the quantity of films they sell do not amount to a "significant" degree. This would be unlikely as no person under the age of 18 is permitted to enter premises in respect of which a sex establishment licence is in force. In Interfact Ltd v Liverpool City Council; Pabo Ltd v Liverpool City Council [2005] EWHC 995 Admin, the Court held that R18 films may only be sold in person at a licensed shop, and not by mail or telephone.

The Council can specify the application form and the supporting information to be provided. When considering the application the Council may assess a range of factors including whether or not the premises are in an inappropriate location, for example near a school, a place of worship or family shopping area. Under the LGMPA82 the Council may also impose limits on a specific "locality" (as defined in Schedule 3) based on the character of the area. The limit may be zero (R v Peterborough ex parte Quietlynn (1987) 85 LGR).

The application may be submitted by a company or individual over 18 and must include the following (Schedule 3):

- Applicants name and address.
- Company details if appropriate.
- Address of premises.
- Hours of opening/operation.
- Fee.

Applications must be served on the chief officer of police and normally be advertised in the local press and a notice must be displayed outside the premises for a period of 21 days.

The Council is allowed to set fees which reasonably represent the costs incurred. This matter has proved very contentious as there is a wide variation of fees. The issue was considered by the Courts in R v Westminster City Council ex parte Hutton (1985) LGR which determined that ratepayers should be relieved of the burden of the cost of a licensing system and that the Court has no duty or power to decide what is a reasonable fee.

Enforcement is covered in Chapter 11 however the main offences in Schedule 3 are:

- Knowingly using or permitting the use of any premises etc without a licence.
- Knowingly contravening a term or condition on a licence.
- Making a false statement in an application.
- Knowingly permitting someone under 18 to enter premises.
- Knowingly employing someone under 18 on premises.
- Failure to display licence.

Firearms Certificates

S1 of The Firearms Act 1968 to 1997 prohibits the possession of a firearm or dangerous air weapon without a Firearms Certificate (FAC). A firearm is defined in S57 as a lethal barrelled weapon of any description from which any shot, bullet or other missile can be discharged including:

- Any prohibited weapon.
- Any component part of a lethal or prohibited weapon.
- Any accessory designed to diminish the noise or flash caused by firing the weapon.

The law (S5) defines a prohibited weapon as:

- Any automatic firearm (except certain 0.22 calibre).
- Any pump-action or self-loading rifle.
- Any smooth bore revolver.
- Any short self loading or pump action smooth bore gun.
- Any firearm which is less than 60cm or has a barrel less than 30cm.

Air rifles and paintball guns typically fall outside of this definition unless they fall into the category of "specially dangerous" ie it is capable of discharging a missile form the muzzle of the weapon with a kinetic energy in excess of 6ft lbs (8.13 Joules) for a pistol or 12 ft lbs (16.27 Joules) for a rifle.

Applications are made to the local police and to gain a FAC applicants must either:

- Demonstrate that they have shooting rights over suitable land.
- Belong to a recognised shooting club.

Clubs will normally admit new members as prospective members for a probationary period requiring a minimum number of visits. Club membership will also require references and a declaration that the applicant is not debarred from firearms use or possession. After the probationary period, subject to satisfactory behaviour and no adverse reports from any source, the applicant is granted full membership. At this stage they may apply for a FAC.

If storing the weapon or ammunition at home then the FAC will include the security arrangements for storing the firearm and ammunition. The Firearms Act does not specify the security excepted other than stating that the weapons must be kept safe and secure at all times so as to prevent unauthorised access, as far as is reasonably practical.

Typically the Police will expect the house to comply with the Security of Domestic Dwellings standard BS8220 and the weapons to be stored in the house in a steel cabinet of a minimum 16 gauge (1.63mm) bolted to the floor/wall and secured with a 5-lever lock to BS7558 1992. Some police authorities also require connection to an alarm system. BS8220 requires a five lever mortice dead lock to the front door. All accessible opening windows should be capable of being locked with a removable key and the rear door secured by mortice lock or slide bolts with any patio doors fitted with anti-lift bolts.

A FAC may not be granted to a person under 14 however there is no minimum age for the issue of a shot gun certificate. The application process will include taking two references and declarations about the medical condition of the applicant and any criminal offences.

Scrap Metal Dealers

The Scrap Metal Dealers Act 1964 places a requirement on scrap metal dealers to register with their local authority, and for second-tier local authorities to maintain a register of scrap metal dealers within their area.

Dealers must register:

- With the local authority for the area where the scrap metal store is maintained or
- In the area the dealer usually resides if there is no store or
- In the area where the place is wholly or partly occupied as a scrap metal business.

Registration lasts for three years, and is free of charge.

The reason for registering scrap metal dealers lies in the potential for stolen property to be passed through scrap yards. Compiling a nationwide network of registers allow the police (who have enforcement powers under the Act) to identify likely locations for stolen property to be found.

Scrap metal dealing is described in S9 of the Act, where a person's business consists wholly or partly of buying and selling scrap metal, whether or not it is sold in the same form in which it is bought or acquired.

Scrap metal dealing is not however purchasing scrap metal as materials for the manufacture of other articles (or as part of carrying on a business as a motor salvage operator). Selling scrap metal as a by-product of manufacturing other products is not caught within the legislation, nor selling material brought for manufacturing but which is sold as being surplus to requirements.

Scrap metal means any old metal, including broken, worn out, defaced or partly manufactured articles made completely or partly or metal and any metallic waste. This includes old, broken, word out or defaced tooltips or dies. The Act goes on to specify eight specific metals and to alloys of the metals.

This licensing regime allows very limited discretion to the Licensing Authority in terms of the manner in which it keeps its register, which must contain mandatory details.

The Licensing Authority can specify what form of application has to be used to register. However, S1 sets out the appropriate details to be specified:

- The dealer's full name.
- The dealers' address.
- The address of any scrap metal stores within that area.

S7 provides that the names and details of partners must also be disclosed, as well as further details of the nature of the partnership itself.

Local Authorities are under a statutory duty to enforce the Act within their area (S1).

Dealers must maintain a written record at each of their scrap metal stores in a bound book, which must be kept for two years from the date of the last entry and must not be used for any other purpose. S2, Scrap Metal Dealers Act stipulates the following must be recorded on receipt of metals:

- Description and weight of the scrap metal.
- Date and time of receipt of the metal.
- The full name and address of the person providing the scrap metal.
- The price paid, if any (either the actual price paid or an estimate).
- The registration of any mechanically propelled vehicle that delivered the scrap metal.

Similar requirements exist in relation to metal dispatched from or processed from the dealer.

Where a scrap metal dealer can show the local authority that the business is part of the business of an itinerant collector, the Licensing Authority after consulting the chief officer of police can make an order relaxing the recording requirements. In the alternative the scrap metal dealer must obtain a receipt from the purchaser of scrap metal showing the weight and its aggregate price, such receipts to be kept for two years and to be produced on demand to an appropriate person (see below). The order can be revoked at any time by the Licensing Authority.

Providing an application is made before the existing registration expires, the record can be renewed for a further three years. It is suggested good practice for local authorities to issue reminders between two and three months before the expiry date and for renewal applications to be submitted one month before the expiry date.

Any changes to the dealers' particulars or the fact that trading has ceased must be notified to the Licensing Authority within 28 days, starting with the day on which the event in question occurs, and the Council must amend the register accordingly.

No fees may be charged for registrations.

10

Statutory Duties

This chapter covers the following premises related laws or statutory duties:

- Fire safety reform.
- Disability Discrimination Act.
- Planning.
- Building regulations.
- Energy assessment certificates.
- Party Wall Act.

Fire Safety

The Regulatory Reform Act 2001 gives Ministers the power to reform legislation which imposed burdens on business. The Reform (Fire Safety) Order 2005 changes all fire safety legislation for non-domestic premises. From the 10 October 2006 employers or owners of premises must manage fire risks and emergencies. All businesses including self-employed and the voluntary sector are affected.

There is a duty on every employer to complete the five actions below and establish who is responsible for fire safety, nominating them as a 'Responsible Person' (RP):

- Assess the fire risk in the workplace.
- Check that fires can be detected and people can be warned.
- Check that there is a safe means of escape.
- Provide and maintain fire fighting equipment.
- Instruct their employees on what to do in event of a fire.

Any risk assessment procedure includes five stages:

1. Identify the hazards such as potential sources of ignition and fuels.
2. Decide who might be harmed and how they may be harmed.
3. Evaluate the risks and decide whether the existing precautions are sufficient. If any shortcomings are identified there must be an action plan stating how the problem is being addressed, including timescales.
4. Record the findings.
5. Review the assessment and revise it if necessary as part of a continuous process which is monitored and audited.

The Office of the Deputy Prime Minister (ODPM) has produced the following Guides specific to the type of premises:

Guide 1 - Offices and shops.
Guide 2 - Factories and warehouses.
Guide 3 - Sleeping accommodation.
Guide 4 - Residential care premises.
Guide 5 - Educational premises.
Guide 6 - Small and medium places of assembly.
Guide 7 - Large places of assembly.
Guide 8 - Theatres and cinemas.
Guide 9 - Outdoor events.
Guide 10 - Healthcare premises.
Guide 11 - Transport premises and facilities.

Guide 6 covers small and medium sized pubs, clubs, village halls and community centres etc. Guide 7 larger venues, (over 300 capacity) and Guide 8 theatres/cinemas etc.

Disability Discrimination Act (DDA)

The DDA was passed in 1995 and amended by the Disability Discrimination Act 2005 to prevent discrimination against disabled people, in much the same way as preventing discrimination on the grounds of race or gender. However, disabled people are also up against what is known as the built environment and transport. Steps, for example, are an immediate barrier to a wheelchair user and from 1st October 2004 licensees and venues should have done their best to remove unnecessary physical barriers. Although occupiers should do their best, they are not expected to bankrupt themselves trying. Some existing buildings may be very difficult and in some cases almost impossible to alter. On the other hand, sometimes a small adjustment can make a big difference.

The DDA is civil law and therefore it is for the disabled person to start an action i.e. someone faced with an unnecessary barrier can take the building owner to court. In blatant cases the Disability Rights Commission has been known to take up the cause but they are more likely to try conciliation first. Licensees have a defence if they can show that they have taken all reasonable steps to remove these barriers.

For wheelchair users those responsible for premises should consider the following:

- Access from the car park, including a ramp if feasible (as a guide max slope of 1 in 12).
- A level threshold at the entrance.
- Sufficient distance between lobby doors (1.57m between door swings).
- Width and turning space (external doors 800mm, internal doors 750mm, corridors 1.2m and turning 1.2m-1.5m).
- Moveable chairs to allow wheelchairs at tables.
- An "accessible" unisex toilet on the same level (new standard 2.2m by 1.5m).
- If you are refurbishing, how about a part of the bar counter at wheelchair height – about 760mm.
- Self-closing doors that have a very low opening force (30N).
- Fire evacuation – try to avoid steps on a fire escape route and have a management plan for anyone upstairs.
- Hotels – at least 1 in 20 bedrooms suitable for wheelchair users.
- Spectator seating – 1% of seating area dedicated to wheelchairs (min 6 places).

For the visually impaired consider these points:

- Contrasting step 'nosings' (eg white lines on the edges of steps).
- Contrasting doorways (people with very poor sight might not see the door).
- Contrast between furniture and carpeting.
- Clear signs with good contrast.
- Menu and price list in large print or possibly Braille.

For the hearing impaired consider:

- Induction loops to aid hearing.
- Canopy over a payphone to reduce background noise.
- Good lighting to allow lip reading.

Each premises is different and a common sense approach is needed. Access audits are available from organisations that will produce a list of changes necessary or licensees can complete the process themselves by preparing their own Access Statement. This document must show that the licensee has:

- Tried to establish the sorts of problem that could arise.
- Consulted with various relevant people, including any disabled customers and the local access officer.
- Looked at ways of solving the problems.
- Costed any building works.
- Established a priority list in the business plan with timescales.

Also note that in landlord/tenant arrangements, (e.g. where a pub manager does not own the property) a tenant wanting to undertake adaptations will need to ask the landlord's permission in writing, pointing out that the works would be to meet the tenant's obligations under the DDA.

The Access Statement could be a defence in Court. The statement may justify why the person responsible for the premises hasn't done something i.e. they have tried to overcome a problem but the ground is too steep for a ramp or the building is listed and permission has been denied.

The long awaited amendment to BS 8300 should help licensees meet the requirements of the DDA. The standard gives advice on the design of buildings to meet the needs of disabled people and is similar in content to Part M of the Building Regulations.

The Disability Rights Commission (DRC) also provides a helpful online toolkit from www.disabilityaware.org

Planning Permission

Planning regulations seek to establish an overall and long term view on development. The Government set out in Planning Policy Statement 1 (Delivering Sustainable Development) that *"good planning is a positive and proactive process, operating in the public interest through a system of plan preparation and control over the development and use of land"*.

The development plan is therefore the backbone of the planning system. Its role is to set out the policies by which all development, from pub extensions to industrial estates, are assessed.

Government policy is laid down in Planning Policy Guidance Notes (PPGs) and Planning Policy Statements (PPSs) which must be taken into account by the Council. Those most relevant to licensing are:

PPG 2: Green belts.
PPG 4: Industrial and commercial.
PPG 5: Planning zones.
PPG 13: Transport.
PPG 15: Historic environment.
PPG 17: Open space, sport and recreation.
PPG 18: Enforcing planning control.
PPG 19: Outdoor advertisement control.
PPG 21: Tourism.
PPG 24: Planning and noise.
PPS1: Delivering sustainable development.
PPS6: Town centres.
PPS7: Rural areas.

Permission is needed to build or extend premises or to change from one "use class" to another as in planning terms this would all be classed as "development".

New "use classes" have recently been introduced with the introduction of the Town and Country Planning (Use Classes) (Amendment) Order 2005 which separates the old A3 use class which included pubs, restaurants and takeaways. The new use classes separate licensed premises into A3 - Restaurants, snack bars and cafes, A4 - Pubs and bars (Drinking establishment), A5 – Takeaways, and finally "Sui Generis" (no use class) – Nightclubs and Casinos.

The new classifications are:

A1 Shops. shops, post offices, hairdressers etc.
A2 Financial and professional services.
A3 Restaurants, snack bars and cafes.
A4 Pubs and bars.
A5 Takeaways.
B1 Business. offices, light industry etc.
B2 General industrial.
B3-B7 Special industrial groups.
B8 Distribution, including open air storage.
C2 Residential institutions. Care homes etc.
C3 Dwelling houses.
D1 Non-residential institutions.
D2 Assembly and leisure including music venues.

In most cases permission is required when changing from one use class to another and since the introduction of the Licensing Act some of the boundaries have become blurred. For instance when does a restaurant become a drinking establishment and when does a pub become a nightclub?

ODPM Circular 03/2005 (Changes in Use of Buildings and Land) states that the Courts have held that in determining whether a change of use will occur the planning authority must consider the existing "primary use" in comparison to the proposed "primary use". Each case will always be a matter of fact and degree, however planning authorities will need to take into consideration more than just the provision of regulated entertainment or the opening times. The "intensification" of a use within a class does not constitute development until its effect is to take the use outside of that class altogether.

The Circular also confirms that any planning permissions granted before April 2005 for A3 use would allow the broad range of uses including restaurant, drinking establishment and takeaway.

The LA03 S182 Guidance states there should be no duplication with other enforcement regimes and the GA05 goes further stating in S210 that the Licensing Authority shall not have regard to whether the proposal has planning permission or not.

Surprisingly there is no prescribed application form, with each Council producing it own form. Councils may also set the number of forms which must be submitted, typically Councils ask for four or five copies. The application must include:

- Application forms.
- 1:1250 OS map.
- Plans and relevant information.
- Relevant certificates.
- Fee.

The certificates which must accompany the application relate to the ownership of the land or building.

The fees are prescribed and they are based on the type and size of application.

On receipt of a valid application the Council will determine who should be consulted and consultees are given 21 days to respond. For most applications the consultation will consist of:

- Site notices.
- Letters to neighbours.
- Press notice (if wider public interest).

Councils must consider the views of any statutory consultees and decisions can be taken within the resolved scheme of delegation. Applications referred to the Planning committee will include a recommendation from planning officers however the committee are not obliged to follow this recommendation. The Council may grant, grant with conditions or refuse the application and if granted the application is valid for three years.

In addition if a building is "listed" then "Listed Building Consent" will also be required for any physical alterations. Old buildings (pre-1840) or buildings of particular architectural or historic value may be listed and categorised into one of three grades (Grade I, Grade II* or Grade II).

The application process is similar to the planning application process however there is no fee payable.

For appeal against a planning decision refer to Chapter 8.

Building Regulations

The Building Regulations are made under the powers of the Building Act 1984, and apply to England and Wales. The regulations provide a minimum standard for new and altered buildings with the law defining "building work" as:

- The erection/extension of a building.
- The installation/extension of a service or fitting (including temporary work).
- Cavity insulation.
- Underpinning.

Services and fittings include WCs, showers, washbasins, kitchen sinks, hot water cylinders, drainage, windows and fires/boilers.

The details are set out as guidance in "approved documents" which outline ways of achieving the standards required. This provides a flexible approach to promote flexibility and innovative design. The approved documents fall under the following headings:

Part A: Structural stability from foundations to roof structure.

Part B: Fire Safety, including means of escape and fire resistance.

Part C: Site preparation and resistance to moisture for roofs, walls and floors.

Part D: Toxic substances and cavity insulation.

Part E: Sound insulation between dwellings.

Part F: Ventilation from kitchens, bathrooms and roof spaces to prevent condensation

Part G: Hygiene provision of WCs and hot and cold water.

Part H: Drainage and waste disposal.

Part J: Heat producing appliances. Measures to prevent carbon monoxide poisoning and fire spread.

Part K: Stairs, ladders, ramps, guards, etc safety on stairways and changes in level, window openings and automatic doors.

Part L: Conservation of fuel and power.

Part M: Access and facilities for disabled people.

Part N: Glazing - materials and protection.

Part P: Electrical safety.

Many simple repair works do not require building regulation approval although structural alterations, installation of services, renewal of windows and most extensions will need approval. From the 1 January 2005, this has included electrical work in homes and gardens or the work must be completed by a "registered" contractor.

Since 1985 certain applicants have been able to choose who provides the Building Control service, namely:

- Council Building Control or
- Private "Approved Inspectors".

In a number of cases they may also choose the application process between a "Full Plans" or "Building Notice" application. As the name suggests a full plans application includes complete details of the proposal and an approval certificate is issued. With a building notice there is no approval certificate and the work is approved on site as construction progresses.

Fees are payable for applications and for councils the fee levels are prescribed in the Building (Local Authority Charges) Regulations 1998.

The Council may approve, approve subject to conditions or refuse the application.

For appeal against a building regulation decision refer to Chapter 8.

Building Energy Rating Certificates

The EU has introduced the Energy Performance of Buildings Directive (EPBD) which requires the UK government to implement a number of significant changes in the law. This includes the introduction of a new Part L of the Building Regulations (Conservation of Fuel and Power), however there are much wider implications for all existing buildings.

The EPBD also requires that:

- Existing buildings, including licensed premises, are certified with an energy rating (likely to adopt a similar rating system as used for new "white goods" such as fridges) and
- The compulsory upgrading of the energy performance of existing buildings when certain works are completed.

In 1997, at the Kyoto summit, the UK government made a commitment to reduce carbon omissions. In 2003 the Energy White Paper set an aspiration for the UK to reduce carbon emissions by 60% and create a low carbon economy by 2050.

The next stage is the rating and certification of existing buildings. When the EU introduced the compulsory rating of white goods the measure had a direct impact on the sales of fridges etc as consumers could easily identify the most efficient units. It is hoped that such a rating system on buildings will have the same impact.

The UK is likely to introduce a national model for assessing buildings which will rate A through to G depending on a number of factors including:

- Heating, ventilation and air conditioning.
- Lighting and daylighting.

- Building fabric and layout.
- Position/orientation including solar gain.
- Building management and use.

These measures will be introduced over the next three years and all buildings will need to be rated when they are sold, let or undergo major refurbishment. The Housing Act 2004 (which also introduces the compulsory licensing of HMO's) includes the mandatory Home Information Pack (HIP). The HIP will include, in Section H, an Energy Report to comply with the EPBD.

Party Wall Act

In 1996 the Government introduced the Party Wall Act in an attempt to reduce disputes with neighbours over building work on the boundary.

The law requires that anyone carrying out building work or excavation close to the boundary must notify the adjoining owner two months before with the following information:

- Name and address.
- The address of the building to be worked on, if different.
- A full description of work.
- Proposed start date.

The notice should be dated and it is advisable to include a clear statement that it is a notice under the provisions of the Party Wall Act.

If agreement cannot be reached with the neighbour then both parties should agree to appoint what the Act defines as an "Agreed Surveyor" to draw up an "Award". If the parties can not agree to a joint surveyor then they both appoint their own surveyor to draw up the award together. The two appointed surveyors will select a third surveyor if they cannot agree.

There is a duty on any surveyor appointed to resolve matters in dispute in a fair and practical way.

11

Enforcement

Introduction

Local Authorities have a responsibility, and in many cases a duty, to enforce the law in relation to the various licences, permits or consents that they issue. As with most matters of law, there are a few exceptions to this general provision:

- The Security Industry Authority is nationally responsible for licensing door supervisors, but local authority officers can be designated to enforce provisions relating to the licensing of door supervisors.
- Local Authorities licence motor salvage operators under the Vehicles (Crimes) Act 2001 but have no enforcement powers, whilst DVLA Swansea registers motor vehicle registration plate suppliers which local authority officers have a power to take enforcement action over.
- Local Authorities licence scrap metal dealers and have no jurisdiction in relation to investigating offences.
- There is no Local Authority enforcement provision in relation to issuing permits for charitable collections under the House to House Collections Act 1939, although this will change with the Charities Act 2006.
- Local Authorities have no enforcement powers in relation to amusement with prize machine permits under S34 of the Gaming Act 1968. This will change from September 2007 with the Gambling Act 2005.

Since the responsibility for alcohol licensing moved to Local Authorities in November 2005, licensing enforcement officers have been able to gain accreditation from their local chief constables (where available) to exercise powers under the Police Reform Act 2002, the Anti-Social Behaviour Act 2003 and the Serious Organised Crime and Police Act 2005. These Acts allow accredited persons to exercise a number of specific powers (including issuing penalty notices for disorder) for offences including:

- Drinking alcohol in a designated public place contrary to the Criminal Justice and Police Act 2001.
- Confiscating alcohol from under-18s, and disposing of it.
- Requiring the name and address of a person who has committed a relevant fixed penalty offence.
- Alcohol sales to, purchase for or consumption by under-18s.

Enforcement is generally the final step in ensuring compliance with regulatory requirements, and will often lead to the imposition of sanctions against the offender, who may either act out of ignorance or a deliberate disregard for the law. Enforcement should be in tandem with ensuring compliance with the relevant requirements by responsible applicants and licence-holders who are keen to ensure their activities are lawfully organised.

Compliance and enforcement are essential components of any regulatory and licensing regime, to ensure public protection and confidence.

Effective Enforcement

It is essential that a Licensing Authority directs appropriate resources towards licensing enforcement in order for it to be effective. What is appropriate depends on the priorities of the authority and the overall resources available to it. However, it should be borne in mind that, generally speaking, licensing fees are available to pay for the cost of administering and enforcing the licence regime in question.

Officers tasked with enforcement responsibilities must be adequately trained in the correct legal techniques, which are outlined briefly in this chapter. They must be able to understand the basic legal concepts underpinning enforcement work, including:

- The difference between legally enforceable and non-enforceable conditions.
- The legislation they are responsible for enforcing, the different offences that may be committed, the maximum penalties in each case and any statutory defences that may be available to an offender.
- The options available to Licensing Authorities (see Enforcement Options, below).
- The points needed to prove the individual elements of the offences.
- The criminal law concepts of standard of proof, burden of proof, reverse burden of proof, hearsay, and documentary evidence.
- An understanding of the relevant provisions of legislation such as the Police and Criminal Evidence Act 1984 (PACE), the Criminal Procedure and Investigations Act 1986 (CPIA) and the Regulation of Investigatory Powers Act 2000 (RIPA).
- An ability to compile accurate, contemporaneous notes of incidents and events.
- The skills to take statements from witnesses and to write their own witness statements.
- The skills to correctly question those suspected of committing offences.
- The skills and ability to give compelling evidence in court or before a licensing committee.

Licensing Authorities need to ensure that they have the appropriate equipment available to allow for effective enforcement. This will include items such as the statutory codes of practice issued under PACE, CPIA and RIPA, appropriate facilities for interviewing offenders and practical items such as note-books for recording evidence, cameras, torches, statutory notices etc.

The importance of good media relations can often be crucial to a successful enforcement operation, either during its execution or at its conclusion, to help publicise the enforcement authority's work and to help deter others from committing offences.

Partnership Working

The modern approach to enforcement is towards partnership with other agencies. This can either be on an ad-hoc or a more formal basis e.g. a formal protocol between the Licensing Authorities, the police, fire service and other partners setting out their approach towards enforcing the Licensing Act 2003.

Partnership working is likely to become more formalised with the establishment of the Local Better Regulation Office announced by the Government in November 2006. This initiative will lead to greater information-sharing between partners, joint problem-solving approaches and joined-up or multi-agency enforcement action where appropriate.

Enforcement Options

Licensing Authorities have a wide range of options available when dealing with non-compliance or offences. Not all of the tools listed in this section may be available for every licensing regime. In some circumstances it may be appropriate to select one solution to deal with an issue rather than work through a hierarchy of measures. What is appropriate depends on the individual circumstances of the case (refer to Enforcement Policies, below).

Contraventions of licensing law can be dealt with by:

Advice - Written advice is normally best, as it provides a clear audit trail to justify later action. This does not always require the offender to take corrective action, but may advise them of where they may be breaking the law; it is usually given for first, minor or technical breaches.

Informal warnings - Normally provided in writing.

Formal warnings - Which should be properly evidenced and sometimes copied to the company secretary or employer of corporate organisations.

Action planning - A joint approach, with clear objectives, a nominated lead and timetables for improvement. The Violent Crime Reduction Act 2006 places joint action planning on the part of a Licensing Authority, the police and the licensed trade at the heart of the provisions for alcohol disorder zones.

Penalty points schemes - Some Local Authorities adopt penalty point schemes for transgressions under specific regimes, such as hackney carriage (HC) and private hire vehicle (PHV) licensing.

Points can be allocated for matters such as failing to display a licence plate on a PHV; failing to report an accident to a taxi within 72 hours; or failing to display a fare tariff in a HC. Accumulation of a certain number of points over a stated period of time can lead to further sanctions. The advantages of penalty point schemes are:

- Provides a clear indication of standards and consequences.
- Consistency in enforcement.
- Provides a clear evidence trail to justify any future licensing decisions/enforcement.
- Proportionate and risk-based.
- Can avoid costly and time-consuming legal proceedings.

Statutory notices - None of the main licensing regimes (such as gambling, alcohol, taxi/private hire, security industry, or animal welfare) provide for fixed penalty notices. Under the Criminal Justice and Police Act 2001 (as amended) a number of minor offences have been designated as suitable for a penalty notice, such as buying or attempting to buy alcohol for a person under 18. Under the Police Reform Act 2002, as amended by the Serious Organised Crime and Police Act 2005, chief constables can accredit licensing officers with the power to issue PNDs.

Some regimes allow for the service of statutory notices – for example, improvement or prohibition notices may be served under the Housing Act 2004 in relation to houses in multiple occupation. Suspension notices under the Local Government (Miscellaneous Provisions) Act 1976 to HC and private hire licence-holders are required to be given in writing.

Compliance and enforcement can often be achieved by the use of other appropriate action. Noise nuisance at night from pubs can be controlled by notices served under the Noise Act 1996, as amended by the Clean Neighbourhoods and Environment Act 2005. Dangerous situations can often be rectified by improvement or prohibition notices under the Health and Safety at Work etc Act 1974, or where appropriate using fire safety legislation.

Administrative sanctions - The GA05 empowers the Gambling Commission to bring prosecutions for offences within the Act, and to apply administrative sanctions. It publishes a code outlining its approach to compliance and enforcement, including the issue of administrative sanctions.

Formal cautions - These are now known as simple cautions, to distinguish them from conditional cautions that may be administered by the police or Crown Prosecution Service under the Criminal Justice Act 2003 (and which has no relevance to enforcement action undertaken by Local Authorities). There is no statutory framework governing cautions, but the significance was described in R v Metropolitan Police Commissioner ex parte Thompson [1997] 1 WLR 1519 as:

> '*A formal caution is not something to be regarded lightly. Records are kept of the administering of cautions…Such a caution, while carrying no immediately disagreeable consequence for the recipient, has potential adverse consequences for him should he be accused of offending on a future occasion. He is more likely than not to be prosecuted for that offence and he will not be able to claim a good character before the trial court. If convicted, the existence of a prior formal caution may affect his sentence. Formal cautions are usually cited after any conviction of a juvenile. In practice they are rarely cited in the cases of adult offenders but may be referred to if they are relevant to the crime under consideration*'.

The administration of simple cautions is governed by Home Office Circular 30/2005, and advice issued in the Director of Public Prosecutions' Guidance on Charging (January 2005). According to the Home Office, cautions are warnings given to adults who admit to being guilty of a first-time minor offence. It acts as a first official warning and deterrent. They may only be issued:

- Where there's evidence of an offender's guilt.
- The offender is over 18 years of age.
- The offender admits to the offence.
- The offender consents to the caution, or is otherwise charged with a criminal offence.

Suspending licences - Some licence regimes allow licences to be suspended as part of the enforcement and compliance process. For example, HC drivers' licences may be suspended under S61 of the Local Government (Miscellaneous Provisions) Act 1976 if the holder is convicted of offences of dishonesty, indecency or violence, or of offences under the 1976 Act, or for "any other reasonable cause". PL and CPC under the LA03 may also be suspended following a review by a Licensing committee where conditions have been breached or any of the four licensing objectives have been undermined.

Some Licensing Authorities take the view that a suspension should not be used as a punishment, but only as a temporary measure to either allow further investigations to take place pending a more permanent decision, or to allow the transgressor an opportunity to put right what is wrong. Other authorities take the view that a short period of suspension is a satisfactory form of punishment allowing the licence-holder to reconsider their offending behaviour. Whichever attitude is adopted, Licensing Authorities should have a clear policy to indicate the circumstances in which they would consider suspending licences, and the periods during which a licence may be suspended. Before a licence is suspended, the licence-holder should normally be given the opportunity of making written or oral representations as to why that should not happen. The licence-holder should always be given written notice of the reasons for the suspension, advice how the suspension can be ended where appropriate, and details of any rights of appeals.

Modifying licence conditions - On occasion, the modifying of licence conditions may assist in ensuring better compliance and provide greater public protection than the other options. This may involve placing more onerous restrictions on a licence-holder to enhance that protection, or even to reduce the regulatory burden to secure greater compliance when this can be done without increasing risks to safety or the licensing scheme.

A licence condition can generally only be modified when a licence is subject to an application for renewal. Some regimes allow for the Licensing Authority to do this of their own volition, although it is recommended that prior consultation is undertaken with affected licence-holders and they are given the opportunity to first comment. In other regimes, such as the Licensing Act 2003, Licensing Authorities cannot review a premises licence and therefore modify conditions unless an application has been made by a responsible authority or an interested party as defined in the Act.

Some regimes however allow for a more flexible approach. For instance under S9 of the Gangmasters (Licensing) Act 2004, the Gangmasters Licensing Authority may modify any licence by notice either with the licensee's consent or where it appears that a condition of the licence or of the Act has not been complied with.

Revoking licences - A decision to revoke a licence is a significant step and therefore should not be taken lightly. Clear procedures must be in place to ensure that the affected parties are given the right to a fair hearing under Article 6 of the European Convention and the rules of natural justice. In most circumstances, a decision to suspend, revoke or refuse to renew a licence gives a right of appeal (refer to Chapter 8).

Reviewing licences - The LA03 and the GA05 are the only "mainstream" licensing functions that allow the regulatory authority to review the operation of the permissions granted under it, and to apply corrective sanctions where appropriate. In the case of the LA03, such an application must be started by a responsible authority or interested party as defined in the Act. The position under the GA05 allows Licensing Authorities to be more proactive, as the Licensing Authority itself may demand the review the licence.

Reviews may be brought following a breach of licensing conditions, a breach of the relevant statutory objectives, or following a conviction for an offence under the Act. The Gambling Commission has a powerful role to play in reviews of premises licences under the Gambling Act but there are no review provisions for permits for gambling in adult entertainment centres, family entertainment centres or for society lotteries.

The conduct of review proceedings is set out in the relevant statutory instruments, and Licensing Authorities should ensure that their licensing statements indicate the approach they will take towards review applications. Some of the matters that may be included are an indication of breaches that may be considered particularly serious, or the sort of evidence that is required in order to justify a review.

Refusing to renew licences - A decision to refuse to renew a licence can be an appropriate enforcement response. This may be particularly so when a licensee has been given opportunities during the currency of a licence to take corrective action but has failed to do so.

Many licensing regimes set out specific reasons to justify this course. These can range from a conviction for certain offences to a refusal to allow licensed premises to be inspected, as is the case under S34 of the Gaming Act 1968. Other regimes, such as the Local Government (Miscellaneous Provisions) Act 1982, allow a refusal for "any other reasonable cause", and licensing decisions must be based on the principles of good administration.

Prosecution - Licensing Authorities generally have the power to bring criminal proceedings in relation to offences committed against licensing legislation. Offences may either be specifically limited to those committed by licence-holders, or may be committed by any person.

Most, but not all, licensing offences, may be viewed as offences of strict liability where no intention to commit the offence on the part of the defendant need be shown. At the same time, enforcement officers should be aware of offences that provide statutory defences, normally where the defendant can demonstrate that they have exercised all due diligence to avoid the offence being committed.

Licensing Authorities that are Local Authorities are also able to institute (and defend) proceedings for a wide range of criminal offences under S222 of the Local Government Act 1972.

Targeted Approach

The need for strong enforcement against those who deliberately flout or ignore statutory requirements has to be proportionally balanced against a lighter touch for those that do comply with burdens imposed upon them.

Adopting an open, risk-based approach to targeting inspections ensures that resources are directed to where they are most needed. Many different models to identify and classify risk exist (often based on some form of point-scoring), and licensing authorities will tend to develop those that best meet their own needs and circumstances.

The announcement in November 2006 by the Chancellor of the Exchequer that a Local Better Regulation Office will be created, together with a review of a number of enforcement requirements, may lead, in due course to the creation of some nationally-consistent risk assessment models.

Compliance Code

In 1998, the Department for Trade and Industry published a voluntary Enforcement Concordat to be followed by local and central government enforcement agencies. The Concordat is based on the principles that businesses should:

- Receive clear explanations from enforcers of what they need to do and by when.
- Have opportunities to resolve differences before enforcement action is taken - unless immediate action is needed.
- Receive an explanation of their rights of appeal.

Over 95% of enforcement authorities have adopted the Concordat, which is available on the web site www.cabinetoffice.gov.uk

Under the Legislative and Regulatory Reform Act 2006, the Government has proposed the introduction of a statutory Regulators' Compliance Code based on the principles set out in the report "Reducing administrative burdens: effective inspection and enforcement" by Philip Hampton in 2005:

- Regulators, and the regulatory system as a whole, should use comprehensive risk assessment to concentrate resources on the areas that need them most.
- Regulators should be accountable for the efficiency and effectiveness of their activities, while remaining independent in the decisions they take.
- No inspection should take place without a reason.
- Businesses should not have to give unnecessary information, nor give the same piece of information twice.
- The few businesses that persistently break regulations should be identified quickly.
- Regulators should provide authoritative, accessible advice easily and cheaply, and
- Regulators should recognise that a key element of their activity will be to allow, or even encourage, economic progress and only to intervene when there is a clear case for protection.
- The Regulators' Compliance Code will apply at the point where

regulators make their policies, rules, codes, and guidance. It will also ensure that regulators give businesses easy access to complaints procedures. A draft Compliance Code was published by the Cabinet Office in March 2006, and will be subject to a period of statutory consultation before it is implemented, copy available on the web site www.cabinetoffice.gov.uk

Enforcement Policies

Most enforcement authorities will publish policies setting out its approach to enforcement. This may indicate how the authority might consider particular offences or breaches of conditions more seriously than others in response to public concerns, or set out a graduated approach to dealing with contraventions. It may indicate within its policy its approach towards cautioning or prosecuting offenders.

In R v Glen Adaway [2004] EWCA Crim 2831, the Court of Appeal held that a trading standards department that instituted a prosecution for applying false trade description (a strict liability offence to which there was a statutory defence) should have had regard to the criterion set out in its enforcement policy. The policy required a fraudulent activity or a deliberate and persistent breach of legal obligations, neither of which had occurred in this instance. The trial judge should have dismissed the prosecution on the ground that it was oppressive.

There is conversely a view that by not having an enforcement policy an authority cannot be judged against its own standards in Court.

Prosecute or Caution

Most Licensing Authorities have a power to prosecute under the regimes that they are responsible for administering, although the Gaming Act 1968 (to be repealed in September 2007) is a good example of where that is not true.

Decisions to prosecute must first depend on the legal authority to institute proceedings, and where this is delegated to officers of the authority this must be clearly minuted.

The decision to institute proceedings should normally be taken by an officer or lawyer independent of the investigation, who can provide an objective analysis of the case to be put to a court. In reaching their decision, they may have regard to the Code for Crown Prosecutors, issued by the Attorney-General under the Prosecution of Offences Act 1985. It sets out some general principles to be considered in every case:

- Prosecutors must be fair, independent and objective, and must not let potentially discriminatory views of the suspect, victim or witness affect them. They must not be affected by improper or undue pressure.
- They must ensure the right person is prosecuted for the right offence, in the interests of justice and not solely for the purpose of obtaining a conviction.
- Prosecutors should provide guidance and advice to investigators through the investigative process, including the proactive identification of gaps in evidence where appropriate.

In coming to a decision to prosecute, two criteria must be satisfied:

- Is there sufficient evidence to justify a realistic prospect of conviction, and
- Is the prosecution in the public interest.

The Code for Crown Prosecutors sets out some of the tests to be considered under these two heads – for example, offences are rarely in the public interest if they are committed a long time ago, or if the offender is now very old or infirm. Most licensing offences (with the exceptions of the LA03 and GA05) must be commenced (that is, the information must be laid before the Magistrates) within six months of the offence being discovered.

A more detailed discussion of the decision to dispose of a case by cautioning the defendant is given above, but Licensing Authorities should be aware that a decision to issue a caution should be made on the same basis as deciding whether to prosecute. The decision to caution can be subject to judicial review and the caution can be expunged if the decision-making process is flawed: R (on the application of Wyman) v Chief Constable of Hampshire Constabulary [2006]

EWHC 1904 (Admin).

In Jones v Whalley [2006] UKHL 41 the House of Lords held it was an abuse of the court's process for a private prosecution to be brought against a person after he had accepted a formal caution by a police officer on the express assurance that, if he agreed to be cautioned, he would not have to go before a criminal court in connection with the offence.

Mixed disposals (e.g. cautions, warnings and prosecutions) may be considered where an offender has committed multiple but unrelated offences as part of the same incident.

Other Legal Matters

In investigating criminal offences, the Licensing Authority investigator has a number of statutory duties that are owed to those under investigation and ultimately to the court. The principle statute in this area is PACE. Through Codes of Practice PACE sets out how police officers and others charged with the investigation of offences should discharge those functions. In most Licensing Authority investigations, these codes will primarily relate to the searching of property for evidence, and the interviewing of suspects under caution.

PACE contains safeguards for suspects being questioned, for example by allowing courts to exclude evidence at trial under S78 where it would prejudice a fair trial. S78 provides that any evidence may be excluded if it appears to the court that *"having regard to all the circumstances, including the circumstances in which the evidence was obtained, the admission of the evidence would have such an adverse effect on the fairness of the proceedings that the court ought not to admit it"*. S78 was drafted in broad terms to allow its application in a variety of situations that could not be anticipated. When an application to exclude the evidence is made, the court will approach the application in two stages:

- Firstly, the court will examine *"the circumstances in which the evidence was obtained"*. This deliberately broad phrase will allow the court to consider, if necessary, the entire backdrop to the evidence and how it was obtained. It is therefore important that officers keep notes in their notebook of the background to the investigation and particular circumstances in which evidence is obtained.

- Secondly, they will consider whether admitting the evidence would have an adverse effect upon the fairness of the proceedings. When considering the issue of fairness, the court must strike a balance between what is fair to the prosecution and what is fair to the defence.

Although S76 provides for the exclusion of confessions, this does not affect the ability of the court to exclude confessions if they meet the test set out in S78. Evidence obtained by a "significant or substantial" breach of PACE or one of the Codes is likely to be excluded, as is a confession obtained by a trick.

There is no requirement for the investigators to have acted in bad faith before evidence is excluded and good faith by investigators will not excuse serious breaches of PACE and the codes of practice. Where there is bad faith on the part of the investigators, this will usually lead to the exclusion of evidence. Investigators should ensure that they are familiar with the terms of the codes.

Officers will also need to understand the importance of keeping and retaining all evidence obtained in their enquiries, in order to comply with the disclosure requirements set down in the CPIA. Where evidence of a personal or confidential nature is likely to be obtained through the use of targeted, covert surveillance against an individual (including the use of human sources), investigators will have to ensure that they obtain authorisation from managers of sufficient seniority in order to comply with the RIPA.

Index

Table of Cases